By George Marshall, author of *Spirit Of '69 - A Skin...*

SKINHEAD NATION

Website Preface

As a lot of people reading this will already know, the first book published by S.T. Publishing was Spirit Of '69 - A Skinhead Bible back in 1991. Originally, a mainstream publisher in London, UK, was going to release it, but after a few months of pissing me about, I decided to do it myself. At the time, I knew sweet Fanny Adams about the publishing game, but it's amazing what you can achieve when a lorry turns up at your front door with a mountain of books and you know every last penny you have (and then some) is riding on the fact that you can shift them.

I wrote Spirit Of '69 - A Skinhead Bible not because I think I'm some sort of expert on skinheads, but because I passionately believed that the history of the cult, warts and all, had to be written from the inside. Before Spirit Of '69, there had only ever been one skinhead book that sought to act as a guide to the skinhead cult – Nick Knight's Skinhead (Omnibus Press). First published in 1982, it was largely meant as a vehicle for photographer Nick Knight's skinhead portraits, but was padded out with a few pages on skinhead origins, music, dress, behaviour and the like. What really makes it worth having though is the section on fashion by Jim Ferguson, something that to this day is held in very high regard by skinheads all over the world, and particularly by those who choose to dress in the original skinhead style. Otherwise, the book was and is very much an outsider's view of the cult, something that is underlined by the patronising mix of sociology theory and tabloid-based drivel.

The idea behind Spirit Of '69 was to offer a view of the cult from within, and one so detailed that it would stand proud amidst the reams and reams of complete nonsense that have been written about skinheads over the years. The end result was a book that covered the history of the cult and its music from the late Sixties to the present day, and one that celebrated the skinhead way of life without dodging any issues or pulling any punches. It isn't perfect, but is now acknowledged as the most accurate guide to the cult currently available, and certainly comes far closer to the truth than countless newspaper headlines have ever done.

Skinhead Nation is in many ways both a companion to Spirit Of '69 and an opportunity to concentrate more on the individuals that make up the cult, rather than the events and music that have shaped its history. The hope is that this website will show skinheads as the individuals they are, and celebrate the skinhead cult as it was in various parts of the world in the mid 1990s. Like Spirit Of '69, Skinhead Nation is far from a complete guide to the skinhead way of life and it's not perfect, but again I've done my best, and if just one person reads this and walks away with a better understanding of the skinhead cult then it has been worth doing.

Like any other group within society, the skinhead cult is made up of individuals. All of them share certain things in common or else they wouldn't have become skinheads, but it is equally true that each and every skinhead brings different experiences and beliefs with them when they join the cult. No two skinheads are the same, and although outsiders would like you to believe otherwise – especially sociologists who dream up theories based on all skinheads being alike – there isn't one type of skinhead, or two types of skinhead, or even twenty types of skinhead. Life isn't black and white, and only the truly ignorant fail to see the countless shades of grey in between.

The media and its cohorts take great delight in focusing on the sensational aspects of the cult and by doing so present a totally false and distorted impression of skinheads. If nothing else, this website will hopefully show that not all skinheads are the racists the media makes them out to be, and that not all skinheads are even remotely interested in being used as political footballs. Of course, there are skins who are racist, but they too are totally misrepresented in the media to the point where buzz words like "Nazi" have lost any true meaning.

The Skinhead Nation website is not interested in defending any political position because politics has nothing directly to do with the cult. In fact, if there is anyone reading this whose sole reason for being a skinhead is to pursue one political crusade or another, then chances are, you haven't understood the first thing about the cult and have no right to use its name. It is equally the case though that every skinhead has the right to hold whatever political beliefs he or she chooses to – just as everyone else is entitled to in a free society. And nobody should be allowed to take that right (or any other right for that matter) away from us just because of the length of our hair.

No doubt this website will raise many more questions than it provides answers, but such are the contradictions that come together within the skinhead nation. What's more, the day they know all the answers and actually start to understand what skinhead is all about is the day to hang up your boots en masse.

Skinhead Nation is based partly on the research and interviews I did while working on the World Of Skinhead TV documentary that was first shown on Channel 4 in October 1995, and also on the six years I spent as editor and publisher of Skinhead Times, a 12 to 16 page tabloid-style newspaper for skinheads which had a circulation of around 5,000 when the final issue rolled off the presses in February 1995. The book version of this website was published in 1996 and is currently out of print. Hence: skinheadnation.com.

It was impossible to tell the stories in Skinhead Nation without repeating some of what was said in Spirit Of '69, but as much as possible, I've tried to cover new ground and write about bands, events and people who for one reason or another didn't get the coverage they deserved first time around.

I now find myself among the ranks of ex-skinheads, having hung up my boots in 1995. I've still got a shaved head and still listen to the same music, and my heart will always be with the skinhead cult which has given me so much. I have always tried to give something back in the hope that the cult will go marching on for many years to come and skinheadnation.com continues in that tradition.

Skinhead Nation is dedicated to anyone who has ever had the bottle to shave their head, lace up a pair of highly polished boots, and walk down the street with their heart pounding with pride.

The Big Apple Bites Back

Saturday, August 13th, 1994. New York, New York. The Big Apple. The city that never sleeps and all that. Dinosaur rockers, The Rolling Stones, are in town to play a series of sold out gigs at the Giants Stadium. Not far from the city, an incredible 350,000 modern day hippies and related simpletons are paying a small fortune to relive Woodstock, 25 years after the original event. It rains and rains, and whether they like it or not, countless soap dodgers are having their first wash in years courtesy of God Almighty.

New York itself is hot and humid, and as sticky as an iced bun. Outside a record shop called Bleecker Bob's on West 3rd Street, skinheads are beginning to gather before heading off to where the real action is this weekend. Oi! band, The Business, have flown in from London, England, to play their first ever gig in the States. There was no media fanfare to herald their arrival. No expensive advertising campaign. But, thanks to word of mouth and the underground grapevine, 600 lucky bastards would find their way to Tramps nightclub later in the day to see their heroes in action.

Already, there will be people reading this who have added the words Oi! and skinheads together and come up with a Hitler Youth Rally. If you're one of those people, think again, my friend. The skinheads drinking beer and fooling around outside Bleecker Bob's that Saturday afternoon would have done the United Nations proud. There were black skinheads, white skinheads, Chinese skinheads, Filipino skinheads, Puerto Rican skinheads, Mexican skinheads. Choose a skin colour and it was there.

This is, after all, New York City, the gateway to the melting pot that is modern day America. A city of 80 different languages. Home to more Italians than Rome, and more Irish than Dublin. And despite what you may have heard or read elsewhere, Oi! music isn't a rallying call for the Fourth Reich and never has been. It's just street punk music at its very best (and worst, depending on the band). Nothing more and nothing less.

If the mugs in the media wanted to look hard enough, they could no doubt find some white power skins in NYC. In New York State it would be even easier. There were probably even a few at The Business gig, but if so, they were keeping very quiet about it. The media has a nasty habit of seeing only what it wants to see though and, despite the large numbers of multi-racial skinheads who walk the streets of downtown New York, even Big Apple journalists seem content to trot out variations on the old chestnut that all skinheads are Nazis and a danger to society. Just like most journalists do the world over. Lazy bastards. It makes you wonder what else these self-appointed fountains of knowledge get wrong.

Away from the ivory towers, some of the skinheads hanging out are dressed very traditionally: button-down shirts, Sta-press trousers, polished boots – the works. One skinhead girl, with her hair in a long feathercut style, is wearing a suit that would have been at home at a Desmond Dekker gig at the local Mecca ballroom back in 1969 Britain.

Most of the skins though are wearing jeans, army greens, boots and braces, and a t-shirt or polo shirt. Bleached denim is a favourite as are football shirts. The Cockney Rejects have a lot to answer for judging by the number of West Ham tops. Oxblood t-shirts are another popular choice, and one skingirl's shirt boasts "American Skinheads - The East End Is Everywhere."

Most are happy to call themselves New York Skins, although within their ranks are smaller gangs like The Uptown Boot Boys from Harlem, The Bronx and Washington Heights, The DMS from Jackson Heights, and The Sunset Crew from Brooklyn. The common bond between all of the skinheads present is the shaven head and a sense of belonging to the greatest youth cult of all time. That, and an awesome collection of beer bellies.

Beers are bought from the nearest convenience store and kept in the brown paper bags they come in. The shop-keepers know the game and open the bottles for you. It's illegal to drink alcohol on the streets, but all the skinheads do it because the bars are either too expensive or don't think a skinhead's money is good enough. The two police officers who ride by on horses don't bother to stop, but on another day they might move you on or fine you for breaking the law. Apparently, their mood depends on the availability of donuts. Later in the day, a skinhead from Portland, Oregon called Pan gets a ticket for pissing in a doorway. Drinking on the streets of America has its drawbacks, particularly if you have a weak bladder.

The talk is of records, gigs, girls, band rehearsals – the usual sort of thing. One skinhead is busy selling the latest issue of his fanzine, one of many voices of the street that gets printed on the office photocopiers of this world when the boss isn't looking. With the mainstream press offering little if any positive coverage to street music, fanzines have really come into their own as the place to look for latest record releases news, tour dates, and the like. A lot of fanzines are pretty average affairs, but there are always a handful in circulation that are truly superb, either in terms of quality or content, or both.

An Oriental skinhead shows off his latest tattoo, and it isn't long before others are displaying their works of art too. Both skinheads and skinhead girls join in, some demonstrating why American tattoo artists are held in such high esteem around the world, and others showing why letting a drunken friend loose with a needle and a bottle of Indian ink usually produces artwork associated with five-year-olds and crayons. Not all skins have tattoos, with some preferring to have no distinguishing marks – a clever move in some circles, particularly if you've always got the law breathing down your neck. At least one New York skin, Noah, doesn't have any tattoos because of religious reasons. He's Jewish.

"When I started going to the shows, it was a great intimidating experience – all these kids with shaved heads, big boots and flight jackets, and I'm just this fat podgy Jewish kid from the outer boroughs. As a Jew, I was kind of nervous of these skinhead people. I knew as much as my parents knew – skinheads are the Nazis you see on TV and that was the end of it. And I assumed that to be true until I started going to these shows."

Passers-by either quickly walk past the gathering, or cross over to the other side of the street, thereby avoiding the growing number of skinheads who are now spilling onto the road and sitting on nearby parked cars. A couple with a baby in a pram actually turn around and head back the way they came – just in time too because everybody knows that skinheads eat babies. Not that the skinheads were paying the slightest bit of attention to who came and went. Unless they happened to be blonde, female, early twenties, with big tits and long legs. Even a few hairies risked getting the piss taken out of them by creeping by, heads down, on their way to the safety of Bleecker Bob's record racks. Nobody died.

Someone jokingly does a sieg heil salute for the camera. On another day, that same photo might appear in an article exposing the "Nazi threat". In another place, the salute might have been meant. Yeah, some skinheads do see themselves as modern day Hitler Youth, but the simple truth is that not all skinheads are Nazis, just like not all coppers are bastards, not all priests are child sex offenders, not all journalists are village idiots, and not all football referees are blind.

New York was actually the birthplace of SHARP (Skinheads Against Racial Prejudice). It was started in the mid-Eighties by three skinheads from the city, namely Marcus (now a tattoo artist in California), Troy, and Bruce. At the time, the skinhead scene was scraping along the bottom of the barrel - you even had black Nazi skinheads. The media feeding frenzy that goes on to this day was already in full swing and so SHARP started handing out leaflets and putting up posters to let people know that, contrary to what the media was saying, not all skinheads are racist.

Initially, it gained widespread support in the city, giving it the momentum to spread throughout the USA and then beyond - today there are SHARP chapters throughout the world. Another organisation, SPAR (Skinheads and Punks Against Racism) also made a brief appearance in New York, but never caught on like SHARP did. Slowly, but surely though, SHARP lost its way in New York. Some say it became too positive, trying to paint skinheads as angels. Others tell you it became too elitist and violent, with only SHARP skinheads being tolerated. Others still say that it was totally ineffective and you are fighting a losing battle if you think the general public is even remotely interested in hearing the skinhead's own version of events. And then, there was the left-wing infiltration, taking it away from its original stance towards the murky world of politics.

SHARP still lives on in New York to this day and has basically returned to its founding roots, but is nowhere near as large or as influential as it once was. If you have grown up in and you are part of the New York skinhead scene today, the colour of somebody's skin just can't be an issue.

"I wear a SHARP patch and I come out to the city," says Pete, who was in the band Vibram 94 until it relocated to Cleveland, Ohio, "and everyone is like, 'What are you wearing that for? Why do you have to label yourself?', but nobody understands that where I'm from, out in the sticks, you have to or you're pinned as a Nazi."

The city has a long history of gang culture, even if today South Central L.A. is the place to be for drive-by shootings and the like. As the mythical murder capital of America (it's actually currently Gary in Indiana, where the murder rate is nearly six times that of New York), a killing doesn't even make the news in the Big Apple, but it will be chalked up on the electronic scoreboard in Times Square that charts gun sales against deaths by shootings. Maybe, one day, someone will actually look at it and see the connection.

Virtually all of New York's street gangs are territory based – the so-called neighbourhood or 'hood, which can be anything from a sprawling housing project to a single street corner. That's been the case since gang warfare first captured the public's attention in the late Fifties when gangs like The Sinners, The Jokers, and The Demons fought for control of the city's darkest streets – a world romantically captured in the musical, West Side Story, but not so entertaining if you were one of the teenagers on the receiving end of a bullet or a blade. Crime and drugs were the driving factors behind the gangs of old, just as they are for the current generation of homeboys.

The skinheads in NYC are a totally different ball game. They come from a gang tradition, but have little in common with other American street gangs, with the possible exception of bikers. Born in the city's Lower East Side when the Seventies gave way to the Eighties and as punk rock mutated into hardcore, the first skinheads could be found hanging around a club called the A7 on Avenue A. There were maybe a hundred or so skins in the city back then, and as the hardcore music scene grew, so did their numbers.

Bands like Agnostic Front, Murphy's Law, and The Cro-Mags quickly developed a skinhead following, and touring helped spread the skinhead cult to other cities. The Lower East Side Skins, or Lower East Side Crew as they became known, were drawn together by a love of music and the skinhead style which was imported and adapted from their British counterparts. It was a hard uncompromising uniform and it suited hardcore perfectly. There was no territory to defend and no drug wars to fight. Just a music and style that gave them a sense of unity and of belonging to something that mattered. From this came the same pride that is shared by skinheads the world over, regardless of what else they may have or may not have in common.

The kids who turned up at gigs at the likes of CBGB's on a regular basis often had nowhere else to go and sometimes had no family worth speaking of beyond their skinhead brothers and sisters. When violence reared its often ugly head, it was usually in defence of one another, the good name of the skinhead cult, personal differences, what have you. Fists and boots were the weapons of choice, not assault rifles and hand-guns.

The biggest battles were in the late Eighties, around Thomson Square Park, New York's squatter ghetto. If it wasn't squatters against the authorities, it was skinheads against the squatters. Little rich kids begging for money in the street while mummy and daddy live in a big house in the suburbs do tend to get up people's noses sooner or later. A boot in the face seemed to do the trick though.

A lot of water has passed under the bridge since the days when CBGB's was a focus for skinhead activity, and a lot of the old hardcore skins are now ten-a-penny hoodlums, but New York still boasts a healthy skinhead scene. Hardcore has more or less been abandoned by today's NYC skinheads to crusty punks, skateboarders, body piercers, and college students, but there are still a lot of good people involved in it, including skinheads. The day after The Business gig, there was a matinee benefit to raise money for the family of a hardcore band member who had recently been shot dead. Agnostic Front, Warzone and other NYC bands played to a full house, but the long queue outside the venue before the gig was home to only a handful of skins.

Hardcore was originally just a development of punk, but today it has drifted more towards metal, and is available in more flavours than Wall's ice cream. Speedcore, hatecore, metalcore, deathcore, queercore, and so on and so on. A lot of American skins still have a lot of respect for the original sound of hardcore though, not least because it was homegrown, and bands like Warzone, fronted by skinhead and ex-Agnostic Front drummer Ray Bies (RIP), remain true to the original hardcore ideals.

The music that has captured today's New York skinhead generation is Oi!, as demonstrated by the fact that The Business were being supported by a handful of local Oi! bands, including The Templars, Oxblood, and Battle Cry. The whole atmosphere of the New York scene perfectly mirrors the excitement and raw energy of the London Oi! scene of early 1981, when everything was fresh and happening and hadn't been ruined by the glue sniffers, the stiff right arm boys, and media hysteria.

Not that Oi! is the only music that skinheads listen to in NYC. The city also boasts one of the finest ska and reggae scenes of today, thanks largely to the efforts of Moon Records and a band called The Toasters. Both were started by an old skinhead from Plymouth, England, called Rob Hingley who went out to America to work for a few months, and has never quite made it back. It really is a small world, but as someone once said, I still wouldn't like to paint it.

Ska in the States has gone from being seen as "a funny little musical genre" to becoming one of the biggest underground scenes, constantly threatening to break through into the mainstream. Hybrid bands like The Mighty Mighty Bosstones have already made it, and if nothing else, American ska certainly offers variation by the dozen on the Jamaican sound of old. Moon's success – The Toasters' 1994 album, Dub 56, had an initial pressing of 15,000 copies – is based on ten years of its bands constantly touring, great support from college radio, and a belief that ska music deserves to be out there, big and proud. Moon even has its own retail shop, currently situated at 150 East 2nd Street, off of Avenue A.

"When I first got here in 1980, there wasn't a scene at all," says Rob, who is known to one and all as Bucket. "Most of the New York skinhead scene really kicked in with the hardcore thing in the Eighties and that translated into ska skinheads. It's difficult to crystallise the difference between the skinhead factions in the US, but the New York skinheads – there's a lot of them and they're pretty cool."

On the way from Bleecker Bob's to Tramps, a dozen or so skins steam into another convenience store, grab a bottle of beer each, and leave without paying. One skin picked up a bottle of American beer by mistake and tries to get the shop owner to exchange it for an imported brand. The owner obliges.

Around a hundred skinheads have set up camp outside Tramps, soaking up the sun and knocking back the beer before the gig. A startled shopper who parked her car in a quiet back street comes back three hours later to find a group of heavily tattooed skinheads using the bonnet and boot as a three-piece suite. Everyone gets off no problem as she fumbles with her keys, praying to God that she gets out of their alive. She lived to tell the tale.

As well as people from all five city boroughs, skinheads have travelled from Pennsylvania, Kansas, Michigan, California, Kansas, Illinois, Hawaii, Canada, and even France to be present at what at the time looked like being maybe the one and only opportunity to see The Business play live on American soil. Such is their standing in street punk circles though that the band actually returned to the States in 1995 and completed a six week tour, playing to packed houses everywhere they went.

The New York gig has been organised by United Front, a non-racist organisation started by three skinheads while serving in the army, in an attempt to unite the American skinhead scene. It puts on Oi! and ska shows, produces its own newsletter, and has no time for politics within the scene.

"By choosing the term non-racist, it shows we're not racist and we're not anti-racist, and it's not that we're on the border, it's just we don't care," explains Bohdan, one of the founders. "We'd rather worry about being skinheads, carrying on the skinhead culture, than worry about who called so-and-so a nigger or who beat so-and-so up because he was white power. You could spend your whole life chasing racists around, but we'd rather concentrate on skinhead. We don't care about the right, we don't care about the left."

Most of those present at the gig are skinheads, but there are also a few punks, and even the odd normal too. A good proportion of the audience is also female which makes a pleasant change. The American Oi! bands sound a lot better than they do on some of the ropey demo tapes that had made it to Europe earlier that year. The Templars, Oxblood, Vibram 94, and Battle Cry all turn in decent sets of hard-edged street punk. The locals have seen the bands countless times and provide a backing choir for both the sprinkling of covers and the original material on offer.

Phil Templar, a black skinhead from Long Island, seems to be a permanent fixture on the drum stool, and even a depleted Pist N Broke from Detroit manage to bang out a few numbers with the help of Perry from Carry No Banners skinzine. While Vibram 94 were on stage entertaining the hordes, Perry was downstairs in the dressing room with Ben and Scotti learning the chords.

With the exception of Oxblood's psychobilly fanatic, Frank Bruno (the real one, not the heavyweight boxer), all of the band members are skinheads, and when they're not on stage, they're in the crowd, dancing and singing along with everyone else. There's no room for rock star egos in this game. Between bands, reggae and ska classics are played.

One of the Long Island mini-skins complains about the price and quality of the beer on sale, and the fact that he can't get served. The barman wants proof that he's 21. He's actually 12. His worries are soon forgotten though as The Business make their way to the stage.

For Oi! fans, they don't come much bigger or better than South London's finest. The Business kick off with Suburban Rebels and the crowd becomes one as the "Us against the world!" chorus echoes around the sweating walls. "You don't scare us with your badges and banners! You know fuck all about heavy manners!"

Real Enemy, Handball, Product, Saturday's Heroes, and other street classics are spat out with the same venom as a sub-machine gun discharging its ammo. Chants of "Skinhead! Skinhead!" fill the air between songs. The Business are superb as usual, even if the band feel they are below par after the long flight over. One poor sod came by Air India so the odd bum note could be forgiven.

Anyone reading this who hasn't heard The Business' brand of melodic street punk should do themselves a big favour and get on down to their local record shop and pick up a CD or two. That said, the chances are you'll have to order them because quality music is no guarantee of shelf space. That's almost permanently reserved for major label acts. Bands like The Business and Cock Sparrer are every bit as good as ANYTHING the mainstream music world has to offer, and it's beyond belief that they don't enjoy the wider success they deserve.

The gig is trouble free - just like most skinhead related gigs. Stage diving and crowd surfing is about as rough as things get. In fact, if you're looking for a good kicking these days, my money would be on going to any local nightclub full of High Street fashions and false smiles. But afterwards and outside, a street fight does kick off between local skinheads and a much smaller group of skins from California. Exactly what started it depends on who you talked to, but the sound of breaking glass, the thud of boot against flesh, and the shouts and screams of those involved lasts a good four or five minutes. A visit to the nearest hospital is on the cards for one or two of the combatants, but nobody is seriously hurt.

Not all of the skinheads outside the venue were involved in the trouble. Some hung around on the fringes, putting in the boot only when they felt it safe to do so. Some just watched. Others were appalled. Skinheads shouldn't fight skinheads said some. Skinheads shouldn't fight anyone said one or two.

"I don't know what happened," said a Brew City Skinhead who had travelled all the way from Milwaukee to see the gig. "All I know is these people got beat up. It's fuckin' bullshit. If you're fighting for a reason that's cool, but when you've got 20 on one that's not a fucking reason. I'm from Milwaukee and in our town it doesn't happen like this. Trust me, if you want to have a fun time, skinheads together, Milwaukee. Milwaukee, fucking Wisconsin."

The following day, ska and rock steady outfit, The Slackers are playing at a small pub on the Lower East Side. A lot of skinheads turn up, but most choose to stand around outside the bar rather than pay to get in.

A black guy walks past, his eyes popping out of his skull. He's either on something very good or very cheap. He starts talking to a skinhead girl called Val, and wonders why everyone is hanging around a usually deserted street corner. He doesn't want to believe everyone there is a skinhead. "But you ain't real skinheads" he says, before explaining that he thought real skinheads were "bald-headed, rowdy, disrespectful, dirty muthafuckas."

"I know who you mean," says Val. "Skinhead girls and skinhead guys, they have the bald heads and the big boots, and the way that you can recognise them in a crowd is that they are burning a cross on your lawn."

When TC, a black skinhead who does a lot to bridge the gap between Oi! and ska in the city, steps forward and says, "I'm a skinhead, I ain't no Nazi," those bulging eyes came close to popping out. A confused space cadet must have woken up the next morning vowing never to touch whatever he was on again.

"You get white people saying, 'Oh cool, you're a skinhead, you hate people'," says black skinhead Phil Templar with a look of disdain on his face. "And you get black people saying, 'Are you a skinhead? You got no respect?' I just say, you don't know what you're talking about. You've been watching too much Geraldo or Oprah Winfrey or something. People don't know shit. They just go along with what's on TV."

Another day, another dollar, on the streets of New York. Music, style, a sense of history and tradition, a brotherhood and sisterhood, pride and passion, laughter and anger.

This is what we are about in New York just as we are in Newcastle. In Berlin and in Buenos Aires. In Moscow and in Montreal. We are everywhere. We answer to nobody, but still have our side of the story to tell.

Ladies and gentlemen, we bid you welcome to the skinhead nation.

Among The Mugs

Like a lot of skinheads, I've got hundreds of newspaper and magazine cuttings relating to the cult. When I was younger, these tales of bank holiday riots, trouble on the terraces, and associated tabloid sensationalism would find their way onto my bedroom wall. Blue-tacked neatly in position, just as they were on countless other bedroom walls throughout this green and pleasant land of ours. A lot of the cuttings have since made it into scrapbooks, but as I'm not the tidiest of people, many more are languishing in boxes waiting for the big day when I finally get around to sorting them out – probably the same day that I'll finally get around to cutting the grass, fixing my juke box, cataloguing my record and CD collection, putting up those shelves...

I was looking through a few cuttings the other day, and it brought it all back to me why skinheads are so hated, so despised, so detested – by people who really don't know me or any other skinhead for that matter from Adam.

Two cuttings in particular caught my eye, both from 1983. The first was from The Daily Mirror, and told of two skinheads who had forced a baby to sniff glue while it lay in its pram in a park in Bristol, England. One of the skinheads held back the baby's hysterical mother, while the other held a glue bag over the baby's face. The second came from The Daily Telegraph, and claimed that four skinheads in Co. Dublin, Ireland, had squirted inflammable liquid in a little nine year old girl's face and had then set fire to her, leaving her screaming in agony and scarred for life.

Such stories about skinheads have appeared in newspapers and magazines the world over. It doesn't matter how much truth is in the stories – Joe Public is going to read them and, chances are, he will take them at face value. And if his only contact with the skinhead cult comes from such media sources, he is going to swallow the media stereotype of what a skinhead is – hook, line, and sinker.

A good few years ago now, The Guardian newspaper ran a television commercial in the UK which featured a skinhead. It started off by showing the skinhead running as fast as he could along a street towards the camera, as if he was being chased. The voice-over said, "An event viewed from one point of view gives one impression..." Then the camera angle changed and you saw that the skinhead was actually running towards a terrified businessman clinging to a briefcase, obviously expecting to be mugged by our friend with the shaved head. And the voice-over said, "Seen from another point of view, it gives a different impression..." The camera angle then changed for a third and last time, and the voice-over concluded, "Only when you get the whole picture can you fully understand what's going on." And you then see the skinhead pushing the businessman out of the way, just in time to stop him from being crushed by bricks falling from the scaffolding above their heads. The skinhead wasn't being chased and he wasn't going to mug anybody. He had run the length of a street and risked his life to prevent someone being seriously injured.

The problem with the media in general is that it rarely shows the whole picture. It has its own agenda of what is newsworthy and what is not – time and space constraints alone dictate that everything that happens can't possibly appear on the evening news or on the front page of a newspaper – and it selects items according to that agenda. And when it comes to the skinhead cult, it has a tendency to only select items from one angle – the angle that shows skinheads as muggers, skinheads as glue sniffers, skinheads as mindless thugs. What's worse is that if a story doesn't quite live up to expectations, it's not beyond certain people in the media to slant the story even further with their own biases, exaggerations, and half-truths. After all, if a story is worth telling, it might as well be a good one.

"Everyone knows the media is run and controlled by middle class people who have never lived in the environment I grew up in, and where skinheads grew up in," claims Symond, an ex-skinhead from High Wycombe in England. "They've no perception at all of how we are because they don't know us."

Gavin Watson, another ex-skinhead from the same town, who has gone on to become both a photographer and an actor, agrees.

"I find the media absolutely incredible because it is totally and utterly based on misinformation and lack of facts by people who have no understanding of the subject they're writing about. White working class males are an easy target. There's never going to be a bunch of football hooligans who are going to get together and take it to court. There's never going to be a bunch of skinheads who'll do it either. We're lower than Bengalis."

The same attitudes among skinheads can be found the world over.

Perry is a skinhead from Chicago, and is half-black and half-Irish-Italian.

"When you walk down the street and people look at you and automatically assume you're a Nazi just because you have a crop and a flight jacket and a pair of boots, that's a big burden to carry around. And I've really come to despise the media because they've really treated the skinhead cult in such an unfair manner that it's really unforgivable. They really have destroyed their credibility with me because how am I meant to believe what they're saying about Bosnia or what's going on in the Middle East when they're giving such a distorted view of what's going on in the streets with skinheads? I think the media is the biggest enemy the cult has ever seen."

Cuttings about glue sniffers or skinheads who set fire to a nine-year-old girl would never have found their way onto my bedroom wall. I'm surprised I kept them at all. For me, the two newspaper articles are about low life scum. They play no part in the skinhead cult that I know and love, and that would hold true for every self-respecting skinhead the world over. Such stories are in no way representative of the skinhead way of life, but it's the tiny minority who are always afforded the oxygen of publicity. 600 skinheads enjoying themselves at an Oi! gig, a ska gig, or even a white power gig just doesn't make the news unless there is trouble.

"The media just repeats that typical stereotype of a muggy bonehead, glue sniffing, granny mugging thug and it's just not like that," says Watford Jon, another ex-skinhead who was well known as a reggae DJ and who still sings with street punk band Argy Bargy. "It's a complete myth. A decent skinhead is someone who believes in himself, knows what he's looking for, knows what he wants, knows how to dress. Just someone who's well sussed, well clued up, knows what they're talking about. No mugs."

"There's a lot of hippies lost in the media at the moment who still carry a sore point for skinheads and that's why the cult reflects in the way it does in the media," adds Steve Goodman, one-time editor of the skinhead fanzine, Chargesheet, and author of the skinhead punk novel England Belongs To Me.

Skinheads aren't exactly angels and very few would actually want to be. Most are more than happy to admit that the skinhead cult has its good and bad sides, just like any other group in society. The media image of a skinhead rarely comes close to how most skinheads view themselves though. In their own eyes, skinheads are the cream of working class youth cults, and if you had to sum it all up in one word, pride would say it all. When you first have your hair cropped and you walk down the street wearing boots and braces, you feel ten feet tall. It's a magical feeling, a feeling of being somebody. No two skinheads are the same, but all of them share that sense of belonging to something very special indeed. Something that few outsiders seem to be able to understand.

"Skinhead's a whole attitude," says Gail, a skinhead girl who lives in County Durham, in the North East of England. "You can't just shave your head and pull on a pair of boots and say you're a skinhead. It's got its own working class beliefs. It's an appreciation of the clothes, an appreciation of the music. I think you've really got to understand the roots to really believe in being a skinhead."

Gavin Watson actually captured ten years of skinhead life in Wycombe through his love of photography. He took countless pictures of his friends during that time, and together they represent a remarkable and rare insight into skinhead life. It's unusual for such a record of working class youth to exist, particularly from the inside, but when his pictures were put on exhibition in both London and High Wycombe they were largely ignored by mainstream art critics. If it had been a ten-year retrospective look at the gay community of San Francisco they would have been falling over themselves to heap praise on him.

Gavin wasn't surprised or deflated. Rejection comes with the territory.

"Some people seem to be able to relate more to an indigenous tribe living in the South American rain forests or Africa than they can to people living just a few miles away. Skinhead culture, working class culture, is as far removed as some of these tribes out in the middle of nowhere. Some people probably know more about what's going on thousands of miles away than they do about a culture right under their noses."

It must be said that there are some excellent journalists out there who deserve nothing but respect. Most people in the media though have little idea of what skinheads are all about and it's little wonder that a lot of skins see the media as the biggest threat the cult faces. They trade in tales of the stereotype skinhead, the thick fascist thug, because that's the only newsworthy element of the skinhead cult most journalists can see. By doing so, they simply display their own ignorance, fears and prejudices, and add skinheads to a long list of people who rank journalists even lower than politicians in terms of trustworthiness.

In the late Eighties, when media interest in skinheads in Britain was quite high, certain skinheads started telling journalists complete nonsense to see if they would print it.

A London skinhead and wind-up merchant extraordinaire called Tim Wells started telling hacks that ska wasn't called ska anymore. It was now called lager house, the skinheads' answer to acid house but with lots more beer. That little lie together with quite a few others appeared in an article about skinheads in The Independent. No doubt some loser will come across it in 20 years time and we will have a lager house revival on our hands.

It's no secret that you get more honesty and sincerity out of a blow up doll than you do your average hack. In fact, I was tempted to write a book called Among The Mugs (with no apologies to Bill Buford) to catalogue the nonsense that passes for journalism these days because if the media truly is a reflection of what is happening in society, then we must all be living in a fairground hall of mirrors. And if any journalist reading this thinks the last few sentences are a touch unfair, well, now you know what it's like to be on the receiving end for a change.

"If there are skinheads out there, and there obviously are, who have taken heed of what they read in the newspapers to become skinheads, and have gone about causing trouble for no reason, then the blame for that lies at the door of the media. It's a monster they've created."

So says Paul Burnley, a long-time skinhead and lead singer of No Remorse. More about them later, but, of course, he's right. If the media wants to continually portray skinheads in the way they do, they then have to take some responsibility for the impressionable youngsters who are attracted to the skinhead look and think they have to go around putting bricks through people's windows because the newspapers tell them that's a skinhead thing to do.

Years and years of media bullshit are also largely responsible for skinheads being seen as foot soldiers for one political extreme or another – and more often than not, for the extreme right. We all have our crosses to bear in this world, and for one reason or another, skinheads have been lumbered with politics. Strange when you know that most skinheads aren't even old enough to vote, and by the time they are, most will have hung up their boots anyway.

"Politics has done most of the damage to the cult over the years," says Gail, who has been a skingirl since the early Eighties. "It's torn it completely in half. It's a personal thing. I've got my own politics, but they're not to do with me being a skinhead, they're to do with me being a person. It should have been left out of the scene right from the beginning and we wouldn't have had so many problems."

It's not just any old politics either. Nobody is interested in hearing a skinhead's views on unemployment, housing, health, and education – the four most important issues facing any society today. No, they just want to know one thing. Are you a "Nazi" or an "anti-Nazi"? And your average journalist (and despite the good ones, most journalists are very average) knows the answer before you've even opened your mouth. Skinheads are by definition Nazis.

"A lot of people don't understand anyway," says Scotti, a non-racist skinhead from Detroit who lives in a mainly black area of the city. "They say, 'You're white, you've got short hair, you're a Nazi, you're a racist, you don't like me because of my colour.' You try to explain, and they still don't understand."

No other youth cult is subjected to this constant association with racist politics. In 1958, teddy boys were largely responsible for the Notting Hill riots. Throughout their reign, they were seen as both racist and violent – one teddy boy was hanged after stabbing a policeman to death during a gang fight – but, today, teds are seen as nostalgic rock n' rollers. In the late Sixties, it was the bikers who adopted the swastika flag, not their arch-enemy, the skinhead, and yet they are always portrayed as loveable outlaws seeking the freedom of the open roads. And then in '76, you had Siouxsie, the Pistols, and other punk rockers using Nazi regalia, but it's put down to the rebelliousness of youth.

All a skinhead has to do though is pick up a Union Jack – the flag of his country if he is British – and he's pointed out as the reincarnation of Adolf Hitler. And even when skinheads aren't even involved, they more often than not get the blame.

"Every time there is a racist attack, the word 'skinhead' will be used by the media," says Emma Steel, a skingirl from West Berlin, Germany. "Skinhead is used as a synonym for Nazi, whether a skinhead is involved or not. No matter what he looks like, skinhead is the word for it."

What was it Billy Bragg used to sing? "Just because I'm dressed like this, doesn't mean I'm a communist."

Well, there are plenty of skinheads out there who would like it to be known that just because we dress like this doesn't mean we're fascists. Patriots, yes, but you can have pride without prejudice, no problem. Not that many people are willing to listen.

"It's more than laughable ignorance," argues Steve Goodman, "because there has been a deliberate manipulation of the truth over the years by politically correct journalists and their chosen causes. They build up and attack whatever they oppose, thereby justifying their own existence and beliefs to the rest of the world. The real shame is those skinheads who thought and think that they've got to be involved in politics – they provide the substance for this distorted crap!"

American television is a case in point. There can't be a talk show on air that hasn't done a programme on white power skinheads. Oprah Winfrey, Geraldo, Jerry Singer, Donahue – they've all been at it. New York TV chat shows regularly flew racist skinheads in from other States to appear on their programmes, while non-racist skinheads in their own backyard were conveniently ignored.

Geraldo Rivera summed the whole chat show circuit up as far as skinheads are concerned. He did a programme on skinheads, and while inviting anti-racist skinheads to come down onto the stage, he gestured over to a group of weirdos with blue hair who weren't even skins to join him. He obviously just wanted a freak show, but Bohdan from United Front and a skingirl also went down dressed in traditional skin gear.

A girl asked Bohdan that if he wasn't a racist, why did he have white laces in his boots and Bohdan replied that he had nothing to prove to her and the colour of his laces meant nothing.

It wasn't long before the audience was beginning to get an inkling of what skinhead was really about, and, of course, Geraldo couldn't have that. He claimed it was all too confusing and cleared the stage. What he really meant was that without the audience getting all hyped up, he wouldn't get high ratings and he would lose money. Geraldo and his like pay lip service to education and go all out for titillation. When a fight broke out in the studio and a White Aryan Resistance skinhead broke Geraldo's nose, it made you feel that maybe there was some justice in this world after all.

In 1993, HBO broadcast a programme called Skinheads USA - Soldiers Of The Race War. No mention was made of the fact that not all skinheads in the USA are white power – the implication was that all skinheads were racists. What's more, rather than provide a truly representative guide to the white power scene, the documentary focused entirely on a neo-Nazi group from Alabama called the Aryan National Front. The ANF turned out to be little more than a group of teenage misfits with shaved heads led by a man called Bill Riccio, who was both a father and big kid figure rolled into one. At one point, Billy is seen wearing a German army helmet, saluting a Nazi flag pinned to the wall in his front room, while he "sings" along to what is, obviously, Irish rebel music celebrating the Easter Rising of 1916. A couple of kids do likewise, while the others sit on the settee, no doubt wondering what the fuck is going on. It's a sad and often laughable attempt to show not only skinheads in a poor light, but also to portray the extreme right as total losers. It is representative of neither.

"The white power skinheads seem to get most of the media attention," says Rob Hingley. "The media's blind because they rarely take the time to come down to a gig to interview people and find out what's going on. They prefer to take their cue from other inflammatory TV shows which portray all skinheads as being right-wing neo-Nazi teenagers – which obviously isn't true. In New York, you can find black skinheads, Korean skinheads, other Asiatic skinheads, Spanish skinheads, white skinheads, and the white skinheads are not necessarily the majority. Obviously, in somewhere like Portland there are more white skinheads because the demographics are such that there are more white people there. It's a mistake to try and typify skinheads as white disaffected urban kids who want to beat up minorities."

A mistake indeed, but one the media is happy to make on a regular basis. If the choice of location is between New York and Portland, hacks will head for Portland because it's a safe bet they will get the story they are looking for, especially if they focus only on the white power skinheads when they get there. But like most places, the skinheads in Portland aren't all racist.

"Portland's really crazy, really violent," says Pan, who comes from Portland, but who also has links with the Carson City mob in L.A. and the Reggae Boys crew that spans the States. "You've got a lot of skinheads fighting other skinheads, but basically it's just reggae boys, ska boys, Oi! boys, some hardcore boys, fighting the Nazis and stuff. It's a small working class town and it just breeds skinheads and has one of the most violent climates for skinheads in the United States. Quite a few skinheads have been killed there, and the violence usually reaches levels of brain damage or being permanently ruined for life. The main crew is the Portland Urban Bootboys, Portland Urban Brotherhood or Portland Urban Baldies, that's like PUB. Ain't nothing but reality in Portland."

"It makes it tough on us because HBO put out that Skinheads USA thing when I was back in High School," says Pete, a SHARP skin, "and for six months the gym teacher was like, 'Hey Pete!', and he'd sieg heil. I caught it from every direction. My parents were down on me, thinking I was some sort of Nazi, I caught it in school, I caught it at work. I caught it all over the place."

The BBC did much the same in England when they made the Forty Minutes documentary, Skinheads, in 1981. They talked to a number of bands about appearing on the programme, including The Business, but instead chose the far more controversial band Combat 84 as the focus of the programme, knowing that they had what they were looking for in the stereotypes department in vocalist, Chubby Chris (who incidentally now runs a bar in Thailand).

Skinheads who aren't racist obviously feel grossly misrepresented by the media's bias. Although obviously grateful for the publicity in a world where all publicity is good publicity, even a lot of racist skinheads don't feel the media portrays them in a true light. Again, rather than give a balanced, objective view of the extreme right, the media only seeks to depict those images that lend support to the media's own agenda, its own prejudices.

"The media only want to portray skinheads in a bad light, and especially right-wing skinheads," says Paul Burnley. "It's an easy target. Who's going to stand up for skinheads with the reputation they've got? No one is going to do that so you can say whatever you want about them, but you can't say anything about gays because you'll have all the MPs who are gay and the pressure groups saying you can't say that. Same for blacks. It's political correctness gone haywire."

Paul Burnley is a leading figure in the extreme right skinhead scene. Whether you agree with his politics or not, there's no denying that he is articulate, intelligent, and offers well thought through arguments. Obviously, Paul is not the only right-wing skinhead who possesses these qualities, but very few ever turn up in the media spotlight. That's usually turned on a thick bastard who can only string two words together – "Sieg heil!"

Politics have wreaked havoc within the skinhead cult since the late Seventies onwards. The extreme right has attempted to hijack the cult for its own ends and has succeeded to a certain degree. Sections of the left wing, and particularly the extreme left and the trendy left, have reacted by branding all skinheads as 'Nazis', a vague term that has lost its true meaning because it is used to describe anyone from a true national socialist to an old granny who complains when she gets short-changed at the Asian owned local corner shop.

The extreme right wing rarely criticise the skinhead cult openly, although you can't imagine rebellious youth cults flourishing under any kind of dictatorship. After gaining the shock value publicity from the use and abuse of the skinhead cult, it's becoming more common for right-wing groups to distance themselves from skinheads though, or to encourage skinheads to grow their hair so that they don't stand out so much – the likes of the KKK aren't called the Invisible Empire for nothing.

Skinheads don't do much for politicians seeking any sort of air of respectability, but they are perfect fodder to do their dirty work behind the scenes. Those on the left wing who continually attack skinheads are the real disappointment. In their lemming-like desire to be seen to be supporting right-on causes – gays, ethnic minorities, AIDS, whales – they seem all too ready to write off white working class people, and especially white working class youth. The tabloid image of a skinhead fits their own world view so sweetly that they are deaf to anything that might suggest they aren't quite as clever as they seem to think they are.

"The reason skinheads are so feared is because they are too true," reckons Watford Jon. "People can't accept that it is such a staunch way of life and that it wasn't a fashion like everyone had hoped for – it's a way of life."

The right-on muppets really make you laugh. They look down their noses at people who read tabloid newspapers, and tell them not to believe everything they read about loony left councils, the trade unions and so on. As if anyone reads the likes of The Sun for its news content anyway. And then these very same hypocritical bastards are only too ready to believe anything that fits in with their own views, especially when it comes to shock horror skinhead stories.

Of course, the skinhead cause isn't helped by people who should know better, like Sham 69's Jimmy Pursey. Talking on national radio, he stated that all skinheads were Nazis – even those who said they weren't. The bloke's always suffered from verbal diarrohea, but he didn't always talk complete shit.

The radio programme went out during September 1992 on the eve of what was later called The Battle Of Waterloo, when anti-fascists fought pitch battles with neo-Nazis near Waterloo Station in London. And as sections of the media were forced to admit, there were skinheads fighting for both causes.

The station was a redirection point for a gig involving Skrewdriver, No Remorse, and Swedish band, Dirlewanger, and an event that anti-fascist groups were determined to stop. During the week before the gig, the media hyped up the potential for trouble, and by doing so virtually guaranteed that there would indeed be violence. In fact, if it wasn't for the publicity generated, hardly anyone would have known about the gig but, as it was, the ranks of both gig-goers and demonstrators was swelled on the day.

There was serious trouble in and around the station, and a number of people required hospital treatment, but little else was achieved. The gig still took place at a pub in South London. So, all Pursey and the rest of the media circus did was contribute to a few people getting their heads kicked in. Big deal.

"If white people have a problem with skinheads, I think, well, you don't have a clue, mate," says Barry, a black skinhead from High Wycombe. "You haven't looked into it at all. It's as simple as that. What you get from black people is an unnecessary grief because you don't expect it, you don't need it. I am a black person so just let me do what I've got to do, just let me get on with it. They don't look at it like that. They look at you as if you're a traitor."

The skinhead cult is trapped in a vicious circle, championed by an unholy triumvirate.

The extreme right wing sees white working class youth, and particularly skinheads, as prime recruitment material.

The media then comes along and distorts this so that all working class youth, and particularly skinheads, are written off as extremists, racists, Nazis, and so on.

The extreme left add to the farce by not only believing everything the media says about white working class youths, and particularly skinheads, but then colludes with it by feeding it with more garbage about us to be repeated on TV shows, in newspapers, and on the radio.

"Both sides just want to use you," says Chris, an ex-skinhead from Columbia, Maryland, who used to be heavily involved in the white power scene. He started the United White Skins in 1991 to contribute to the fight for race and nation as he saw it, but he has since completely finished with white power politics and the skinhead cult. "The far left just want to use skinheads as scapegoats just like the Klan wanted to use skinheads to do their dirty work."

The worst offenders are those people who not only put racism at the top of their agenda, but who also seem to think it is the only issue of the day. That in itself isn't actually the problem. If they've got nothing else to worry about in their lives, good luck to them. But when they start ramming it down other people's throats to the exclusion of everything else, then you begin to wonder about them, particularly when white on white violence doesn't seem to bother them, but the thought of white on black violence has them out in the streets. It's also a bit unlikely that you'll take lectures from people who abhor racist violence and yet see IRA terrorists and their kin as romantic freedom fighters, as is the case with The Socialist Worker's Party, the prime movers behind the Anti-Nazi League.

The likes of the Anti-Nazi League are very good at pointing the finger at skinheads. Your average black or Asian in this country though has far more important things to worry about than whether or not the BNP has a bookshop in Bexley or how many people picketed a white power gig, and that's why so few of them bother to go on ANL marches.

Most anti-racist and anti-fascist activists in Britain are in fact white, and the reason they devote so much time and energy condemning skinheads is presumably because their experience of racism rarely goes beyond what tabloid headlines and their own propaganda tells them.

Obviously, that's not true of all anti-fascists or even all ANL members, but to varying degrees, it hits the nail on the head for a large number of people within the badges and banners movement.

The same is true in the USA. With a population of over 250 million, it's safe to say that the only contact most blacks and other minorities have with white power skinheads is through the crap they read about in their daily newspaper or remember from HBO's Skinheads USA.

Of course, racism is alive and well in the land of the free, but to focus so much media and anti-racist attention on skinheads takes the spotlight away from the root causes of racism and allows the vast majority of racists to go unchallenged.

Racism didn't start with the coming of the skinheads and it won't stop when the last skinhead hangs up his or her boots. Skinheads are as racist as society is in general – sometimes more so, sometimes less – but those who continually point the finger at skinheads are no better than those racists who blame immigrants for everything. Both views are based on ignorance and bigotry. Simplistic answers for a complex world.

"You are just living an easy life by scapegoating skinheads because then you can look in the mirror and say I am not a racist because I don't have cropped hair," says Emma Steel.

The way some people go on, you'd think skinheads were from outer space, bald aliens from a far away planet. These are the same people who think all skinheads are glue-sniffing thickos who mug old grannies. But skinheads don't give up citizenship of the human race when they shave their heads and wear big boots, and just like everyone else in this world, they have the right to think, believe, and do whatever they want – as long as such actions don't infringe on the right of others to think, believe, and do whatever they like.

If some skinheads are racist, that's their choice – you don't have to be racist to support the rights of others to hold racist beliefs. The media's focus on them, to the almost total exclusion of skinheads who aren't racists though, gives a totally false picture of the skinhead cult as it is today.

"The media wants to portray all skinheads as racist," says Graham, a skinhead from Newcastle. "If you've got boots on and short hair, you're a racist. If you've got boots on and you've got long hair, there's nothing wrong with you. The shorter your hair gets, the more racist you're going to become – and that's just not right. The length of your hair determines your tolerance of immigrants?!?"

Skinheads Against Racial Prejudice (SHARP) was originally started in a bid to combat this media bias, and it has enjoyed a small level of success in various areas. Certainly, since its birth, the media has been more likely to give some coverage to non-racist skins, but it is like a drop in the ocean compared to the negative coverage the cult receives. And even when talking about non-racist skins, the same old nonsense gets trotted out.

"I've read the articles on skinheads in magazines," says Ally, a skinhead from New York, "and they always say that even the skinheads who aren't racist are hoodlums, they'll rob you, eat your babies…"

This has led to disillusionment with having any contact with the mainstream media, and growing numbers of non-racist and anti-racist skinheads see no reason to have to explain themselves to journalists or anyone else. Nobody expects journalists to walk about with Journalists Against Racial Prejudice t-shirts on so why should skinheads? What's more, very few skinheads live and breathe for politics. Those skinheads who do pledge allegiance to one cause or another still have a life beyond it. You'd have to be a very sad bastard if you didn't. But for the media, you would think that the only aspect of their lives were their political beliefs. It's the equivalent of thinking professional footballers only exist for 90 minutes every Saturday afternoon, or that Irish people have no other dimensions to their lives beyond the Protestant and Catholic faiths.

This constant focus on just one issue, this blatant tunnel vision, can't possibly deliver the whole picture, but our beloved media blunders on regardless. SHARP too has fallen foul to this media obsession with politics. By standing up and saying you are a SHARP skin, Mr. Journalist assumes you must be against fascism and therefore a political creature of the left. That's no doubt true for some SHARP skins, and others who have tried to use SHARP for political ends, but it was never the intention of its founding fathers. The original SHARP logo had the American flag on it purposely to show pride without prejudice.

"A lot of people take SHARP as a political thing, but it was never meant to be politically motivated," says Paul Jameson, editor of The Skinhead fanzine and organiser of regular ska and soul nights in the North East of England. "It was just a statement that we're not racists. Simple as that really."

"When SHARP first started in New York it was an excellent idea, but unfortunately the way it has been put into practice here and in other places, it became a left-wing political movement," says Perry from Chicago. "At this point in the skinhead movement's history, I don't really see why it's needed. I don't see why I should have to wear a SHARP patch to prove I'm not racist. The general public doesn't really like us anyway so, why bother to impress them with something like that? The best development I see in the cult today is the whole non-political movement, the fact that skinheads are dropping politics generally. Like, no racist element, no SHARP, and skinheads are just interested in being skinheads. And I see that aspect really growing."

It is totally ridiculous that skinheads are defined in political terms largely so that people can make head and tail of a movement that has allowed the media to dictate that all skinheads can be defined in purely political terms. That is absolute bollocks. And the sooner more skinheads stop playing the media's petty games and say they are skinheads – pure and simple – the better off we will be.

"There are only a few skinheads in the world and I think we should fucking get together, hang out, get rid of politics," argues Asian Chris from New York. "I would say to the Nazis, tell the fucking Ku Klux Klan or whoever else hires them to be grunts, to just drop them. They could think for themselves. I would welcome you as a brother as long as you don't put your politics onto me."

"Skinheads have been crucified for the sins of others," says Pan from Portland. "It's hard to break the stereotype because people will always think of you in a certain way."

Neil, who has been a skinhead since discovering Madness in 1980 has a story that captures the media's blinkered vision perfectly.

"In the local paper in Hartlepool, there was a girl who had her head shaved for charity and then a few weeks later, she was up in court for some reason and the headline was SKINHEAD GIRL IN COURT. They'd covered the story about her getting her head shaved for charity a couple of weeks before and yet the moment she's in trouble they said she was a skinhead. It's unbelievable!"

The same sort of thing appears somewhere in the world on a weekly basis.

"Just the other day in The Evening Times, a young kid was called a skinhead, but he was obviously just a little guy going out mugging people," says Marc, a Glasgow skinhead and reggae DJ. "Anybody and everybody who crops their hair is a skinhead if you believe the newspapers, which is pretty outrageous if you're walking down the street and somebody wants to have a go at you because of that."

The mainstream media will no doubt continue to rubbish the skinhead cult, but more than 25 years after the cult first appeared in the council estates of Britain, there are still skinheads around with the determination to keep the faith. Not all of them are racists, and very few of them are mindless thugs on glue. The real mugs are those who can't see past their own prejudices to discover that for themselves. It's not just skinheads who think they get a raw deal from the media – everyone from Hell's Angels to Catholic priests seem to think likewise. The irony though is that the constant and often unjustified attacks on the skinhead cult have just made it all the more stronger.

"Once you've been involved in the skinhead cult, there's nothing like it," says Shaun, a Folkestone skinhead who was until recently a member of local ska and reggae outfit, Intensified. "Perhaps because we're attacked so much by the press, by the media, by other people's attitude, we stick together far more than any other group."

Bring Back The Skins

Back in 1969, following a gig in Birmingham, reggae legend Laurel Aitken found himself being arrested and remanded in custody until the following Monday. He had fallen behind on his payments for a paternity claim, and was facing a £200 fine or six weeks of prison food. The only person he could contact to help him was the owner of Pama Records who duly arrived with the money – to get him out – and a recording contract. Laurel had little choice but to sign on the dotted line, and so began his fruitful association with Pama, and, in particular, its Nu-Beat subsidiary.

The story of Jamaican music is littered with as many such tales as it is classic songs. Thanks to a whole host of reasons, from bad business deals to a largely apathetic music press, Jamaican music also boasts far more than its fair share of unsung heroes. And if everybody played by the same rules, the name of Laurel Aitken would be up there in bright lights beside those of Bob Marley, Jimmy Cliff, and Desmond Dekker.

Although born in Cuba in 1927, Laurel emigrated to Jamaica with his family when he was eleven years old, and quickly became involved in the local music scene – busking in the streets, entertaining tourists as they stepped off the cruise liners, and singing in the numerous and very popular talent shows of the day.

By the late Fifties, Laurel Aitken was one of Jamaica's best loved recording pioneers, having been the first local artist to top the JA hit parade with Little Sheila / Boogie In My Bones (R&B), a single that remained in the charts for over a year. Such success brought him to England in 1960, where he went on to record hundreds of tracks, including Mary Lee for the newly-formed Melodisc label and Boogie Rock, the first release on the now legendary Blue Beat label.

He continued to work throughout the Sixties, including spells as a recording artist with Ska Beat, Dice, EMI, and Graeme Goodall's Rio label, but it was with reggae that he was to have arguably his finest hour. Songs like Landlords And Tenants, Jesse James, Scandal In A Brixton Market, and Pussy Price – all of which appeared on Nu-Beat during 1969 and 1970 – are classics of the era and are guaranteed to pack any dance floor at skinhead reggae dances to this day. In addition, Laurel emerged as one of the UK's leading producers of reggae music, and was much sought after, not only by Pama, but also by their much bigger rivals, Trojan.

Although receiving little to no chart action in the UK (he came closest with the release of another gem, It's Too Late on Trojan in '71), Laurel was selling thousands upon thousands of records at the time. This was true of other reggae artists too, but since most of the sales were through small independent shops, they were not included in the returns that would have given them the chart success and radio airplay they most certainly deserved.

It's interesting to note that the music press showed next to no interest in Jamaican music at the time, dismissing most of it as "crude" and "boring", and radio stations rarely played it until Trojan smashed its way into the charts towards the end of 1969 with a more commercial reggae sound.

Trojan's success was very much on the back of the base support afforded to the music by the West Indian communities of the day and by the growing hordes of skinheads who could be found dancing away to the sounds of Jamaica at ballrooms and youth clubs throughout the country. Songs like Symarip's Skinhead Moonstomp (Treasure Isle), Skinhead Jamboree, and Skinhead Girl (all to be found on the band's Skinhead Moonstomp album which has recently been re-issued as a CD by Trojan, complete with original sleeve featuring a black and white shot of Blackpool skins), Skinhead Revolt by Joe The Boss (Joe), Claudette's Skinheads A Bash Them (Grape), and Laurel's own Skinhead Train (Nu Beat) paid tribute to the fact that it was the skinheads who gave reggae the leg up it needed to reach the mainstream music market.

"I used to play a few places back then and you'd see skinheads on the scene," remembers Laurel. "You used to see a few in the dances, and it just grew. I've been having a skinhead haircut since the Sixties so seeing skinheads coming into the dances with their short hair didn't mean anything to me. I used to be a skinhead and I still am," he jokes, as he takes off his trademark pork pie hat and displays a bald head.

Laurel continues to perform to this day. Even at the grand old age of 68, live on stage he is unbeatable, a superb entertainer. What's more, he displays more stamina than most of the young pups in the audience when it comes to dancing around. His popularity today though is largely and sadly confined to the underground ska scene where he is given the respect a man who is known as the Godfather Of Ska and the High Priest Of Reggae deserves.

In fact, most of today's commentators on the reggae scene should be ashamed of themselves for not giving artists like Laurel credit for their contribution to Jamaican music.

"Whenever I do a show, if I see skinheads, I know I'm going to have fun. If I'm in the dressing room, resting or talking, I always ask if there's any skinheads in the audience, and if they say quite a lot, it makes me happy. The skinheads support the music and if someone supports you, you've got to like them. When I play ska, there's like two black guys there and the place is packed with white kids. A skinhead in Germany told me he'd seen me six times at gigs – if a black guy sees you once, you're lucky."

Back in 1961, a 17-year-old white youth by the name of Alex Hughes found himself at a blues party in a London cellar, listening to Jamaican music for the first time, and enjoying his first ever taste of Red Stripe beer. The sounds being played were by artists like Derrick Morgan and Laurel Aitken and little could he have known then that he would not only go on to work with such musical legends – he was actually Laurel's bodyguard for a period in the Sixties – but would eventually join them as a reggae great in his own right. As the Sixties picked up steam, Alex Hughes did a variety of jobs, including professional wrestling, debt collecting, and working on the doors of various London clubs, and in particular The Ram Jam Club which regularly had 1,800 punters through the door despite selling no alcohol. As a bouncer, he was in as good a position as any to witness the birth of the skinhead cult.

"The first time the skinheads came to right was during the mod time really, going back to the days of Geno Washington and the mods and rockers. Out of that evolved the whole skinhead thing. All of a sudden, the hair became shorter. Obviously, I had my hair cut short at the time because of the size I was and I was also a wrestler, putting a mask on my head and things like that. It was the mid-Sixties when I started to see them, probably about '66, but by '68 - '69, it was rampant. Bank holidays were the big thing – you could go to Margate and see them all milling around. But in fairness, when they talk about the trouble, I've seen the press making them run up and down the beach, taking photographs and saying run this way, run that way. And then three days later you'll see it on the front of the paper – SKINHEADS RUN RIOT."

From working club doors, Alex graduated to working behind the decks, and eventually started his own sound system. Weighing in at 22 stone at the time, and being a frightening looking character, he borrowed a name from a Prince Buster track and called it the Judge Dread Sound System. The way to make a name for yourself as a sound operator was to have Jamaican imports that nobody else had, so the newly-christened Judge Dread would make regular trips down to Sheerness to buy records straight off the banana boats. He became more involved in the reggae music scene, and when he moved from London to Kent, the Judge started promoting bands too. His biggest coup at the time was booking another skinhead favourite, Desmond Dekker, to play when he was at number one in the British charts with The Israelites (Pyramid). Previously, Alex had been the first white man Desmond had really met because Alex picked him up from the airport when he first visited Britain.

"I came down to Snodland when my family moved down and I came across this little picture house-cum-bingo hall. There was a few discos in there and I decided to elaborate on that and so brought down the Coxsone Downbeat sound system and started having a few dances and things like that. After a while, I put on a few groups. The first one was The Coloured Raisins at the start of 1969, and at that time people in the area hadn't really seen black people before. So I not only introduced them to reggae in this part of the world, but black people as well. Then I had The Rudies down here, all nighters, other sounds like Neville The Musical Enchanter and then the ultimate was Desmond Dekker when he was at number one. You just couldn't move. If you can imagine, number one in the charts, 1969, the streets were packed. After that the Savoy became quite famous in the area, people travelled from miles away, and I had a few groups booked. And then one day, the police turned up and there was a massive drugs raid and that was the end of the Savoy as we know it!"

By the end of the year, the Judge was working for Trojan Records and its artists booking agency as a debt collector. It was while working for Trojan that he decided to take the B side of one of the records he used to play, Little Boy Blue, and go into the studio and record a demo. It only cost him seven or eight quid and was never intended for release, just for his own benefit. One day though, he was in the Trojan office and he was playing the demo to the band Greyhound when the managing director walked in. The MD asked if the song was one of theirs – at the time Trojan were releasing an amazing 40 or so singles a week – and when he heard it was Alex, he suggested releasing it.

Prince Buster had scored a massive underground hit with his Big Five, and to capitalise on that success Judge Dread's debut single was re-named Big Six and released on the Big Shot label in 1972. It was an instant hit, selling over 250,000 copies in the UK, mainly to the ethnic market – and amazingly enough, it charted in Jamaica too. Most people assumed that Judge Dread was black and when Trojan took him to an EMI sales conference and they saw he was in fact white, it helped secure a distribution deal that would see Big Six reach number 11 in the charts without any radio airplay whatsoever.

Judge Dread then took the art of rude reggae to new heights, with a string of top thirty hits including Big Seven, Big Eight, Jo T'Aime, and The Winkle Man. Like all Judge Dread releases, they were instantly banned by radio stations because of their saucy lyrics, but that just added to their appeal and helped guarantee their success – although the powers that be didn't always acknowledge this success, thanks to pressure from the nation's moral guardians like Mary Whitehouse.

"Big Seven was selling something like 70,000 copies a day and should have gone straight in at number one, but got no higher than number five."

In 1973, following his appearance at the Ethiopian Famine Disaster concert alongside Bob Marley and Desmond Dekker, Judge Dread released a cover of Clancy Eccles' Molly as a charity record to raise further funds. Incredibly, it too was banned by radio stations because of the Dread connection – it was obviously more important to keep the Judge off the airways than it was to help feed the starving millions. Eleven years on though and the very same radio stations were falling over themselves to promote the Band Aid project. Such is the sick world we live in.

By the mid-Seventies of course, the skinhead cult had hung up its boots en masse, but it certainly hadn't been forgotten by Judge Dread. In 1976, he released his Last Of The Skinheads album on Cactus. On it was the classic ode to days gone by and a demand to return to them in the shape of the song, Bring Back The Skins. It remains arguably the finest reggae cut in honour of the cult ever released.

"I decided to write that song, not knowing at the time that it would become the skinhead national anthem. You can forget your Skinhead Moonstomps because Bring Back The Skins actually depicts what it was all about. The days when people would go down the Palais, and probably they would have a fight and dance to reggae all of the night. The whole way of life was more permissive then too so of course you'd blag a bird, so the song actually relates to what went on in '69. The greatest thing about it was that a few years later, the 2 Tone thing came along and the whole thing was revitalised again."

The Judge remained both a recording and performing artist until his death in 1998, and like your Laurel Aitkens and your Desmond Dekkers and your Derrick Morgans, still commands a healthy skinhead following, not just here in Britain, but throughout the world.

In fact, it's actually quite ironic, but if you want to know about the true greats of reggae history today, you'd be better off asking a skinhead than a black kid with Jamaican roots.

Chris Prete, who runs The Official Trojan Appreciation Society as well as supplying the label with top notch release projects and sleeve notes to match, is one such skinhead who is a walking encyclopaedia on the subject. Chris first became a skinhead when he was 11 or 12 years old, mainly because all of his mates were skinheads and he liked the sharp, clean image.

"There weren't many people who weren't skinheads or who didn't have long hair. You were either one or the other, or at least that's how I saw it at the time. And, in London, it seemed to be mainly skinheads."

Chris and his mates would imitate the older kids who were also skinheads, roaming the local streets in gangs named after pubs, street corners, and the like – the Acre, the Estate, the Queensbury. It was the older skins who first introduced him to reggae – Derrick Morgan's Tougher Than Tough was one of the first records Chris heard – and he has been captivated by the music ever since. His Trojan collection boasts over 1,000 singles and 400 albums – he also had a lot of Pama releases too, but sold them to concentrate on his first love, Trojan. There are plenty of skinheads out there who would give their right arm for a tenth of the sounds Chris keeps neatly sorted by label, from Attack to Upsetter, the latter of which he ranks alongside Downtown and Trojan itself as the top names in skinhead reggae. Personally though, he rates the Duke Reid and Treasure Isle subsidiaries as the icing on the Trojan reggae cake.

"To me skinheads and reggae go together. You can't separate them. It's a basic music, simple and not complicated. It's got a hook with the bass beat, and once you start getting into the music, it's hard to walk away from it. The deeper you dig, the more good things you discover. It really is amazing that so much good music has come out of a small island like Jamaica."

It's not just the original skinheads who feel this way about Jamaican music. It is as popular today among skinheads as it has always been.

"It's hard to describe," says Jacquel, a skingirl from Edinburgh in Scotland who now lives in London, "but it's a really good feeling if you hear a good song and you really get into the rhythm and want to get up and dance. It's something that affects you, and that's why I like reggae and rock steady because it touches your soul."

Toast, a skinhead from Ramsgate who produces Tighten Up skinzine agrees.

"I think it should be remembered that skinheads put reggae into the British charts. If it wasn't for skinheads and the movement in '68, '69, I don't think reggae would have made it into the charts. Maybe Bob Marley wouldn't have got to where he got to if it wasn't for the white working class youth."

Another one-time skinhead who has since devoted his life to the appreciation and celebration of Jamaican music is Gaz Mayall, son of blues man John Mayall. Gaz is not only the proud owner of one of the largest collections of Jamaican vinyl anywhere in the world, but for over a decade now, he has been willing to share its joys at his weekly Gaz's Rockin' Blues, London's longest running club night (currently to be found at St. Moritz in Wardour Street every Thursday night).

"Skinhead was a fashion thing, it was a music thing, it was about dancing, and it was about sex. You'd go to a party, put a sound system in and buy a load of beer, and all the girls would be looking at the boys, and all the boys would be looking at the girls, and within ten minutes you'd have a big fat skinhead chick sitting on your lap! You'd be listening to Big Five and your own big five would be right there! 99 ½% of all the people who were skinheads between '68 and '71 have some great memories. It was just the vibe of the times. Great music and great style."

When you talk to anyone who was a skinhead during the original era, the memories come flooding back as if it was yesterday.

"I was the first skin in the area," says Stuart, who brought the skinhead fashion to Bridlington on the East coast of England from his native Leeds. "I got quite a few strange looks at first because everyone had long hair, permed hair, and was into Mungo Jerry, that kind of music, and I was into reggae and all the opposites. Then I got involved with two scooter clubs from Leeds, one called The Lulus and the other The Incas, and after a few years, the full length of the seafront was full of scooters with the mirrors on, cradle back rests. There were hundreds of skinheads here in the summer, but in the winter there was maybe a dozen."

At the time, most people no doubt thought that Stuart and the other Bridlington Skins would amount to very little, but nothing could be further from the truth.

"People marked you as a villain or a con or a thug, that sort of thing. Since then I've had my own pawnbroker's shop, I've had a jeweller's shop, I've got my own 44 bedroom hotel with a pub, cabaret club, I've been a promoter, sang on the Motown Show with The Temptations, The Four Tops, Judge Dread... A lot of my friends are now in business, they've all got on, and they've all been skinheads. They're as good as anyone else. The media treat skinheads wrong, just like they treat a lot of people wrong. People should go by personal value, not face value. You should never judge a book by its cover because there's good and bad in all."

It's been over 20 years since Stuart was a skinhead, but he still sees himself as belonging to the skinhead cult, almost as if it is something that stays in your blood forever. A feeling shared by many others who have given part of their life to being a skinhead.

I once went to a work's party, and it was a smart affair so I turned up in a tonic suit, loafers and Bennie. Anyway, this lady came up to me and said, "Is that a Ben Sherman shirt?" She was in her early forties, but from the collar alone could tell what make of shirt it was. It turned out that her husband, a bank manager no less, had been a skinhead first time around, and still refused to throw out his old shirts even though they no longer fitted him. I then spent the rest of the evening drinking and talking with him, as he reminisced about skinheads in his home town of Gateshead.

I was also stopped by a policeman once, and just thought it was yet another Noise Up Skinheads day. But no, this bobby had seen my Trojan Skins patch, and couldn't stop talking about how he used to be a skinhead into reggae, how he collected Trojan, joined the Trojan Appreciation Society, still had the members' medallion, and so he went on.

As Stuart says, "You never really get out of it. It's you."

Not so long ago, Stuart appeared on a TV programme, over an incident where he had caught one of his employees stealing from hotel rooms. Knowing that the police would do very little about it, Stuart had set up a video camera in a room and caught the bloke in the act. Then together with his son, Stuart grabbed hold of the thief, took him to the basement, and "extracted a confession". Locals who are equally fed up with nothing happening to petty criminals saw Stuart as a vigilante, and he was praised in the local paper. However, the TV documentary tried to make him out as a thug who took the law into his own hands – as if the toerag he'd given a job to didn't deserve a good slapping.

Just as Stuart still sees part of himself as belonging to the skinhead cult, very few skinheads reading this will think he did wrong. You don't let people shit on you and get away with it.

"I consider myself a skinhead even although I don't look like one now," says Rob Hingley, echoing the feelings of countless ex-skins. "I looked like one in the past, but I think it's more of a mental state of being in a movement that's been around since 1967, and being proud of your working class heritage, being clean and tidy, and having respect for people around you. It's a proud badge of working class courage, that's how I see it. I might not look like a skinhead anymore, but it's in my heart."

Graham, another original skinhead from Bridlington, has never hung up his boots. To this day, he can be found working the doors of nightclubs with a cropped head and wearing his crombie coat and boots.

"I first became a skinhead in 1970. It was after we'd seen some of the older lads like Stuart and we thought, that looks good. We couldn't afford the Doctor Marten boots or the Ben Shermans so we just made do with army boots, granddad shirts, and as we could afford it, we bought the clothes. You felt ten feet tall when you put your boots on, you felt really good, felt somebody."

Brian Kelson has also remained true to the skinhead faith more or less since first signing up in 1970.

"It was work all week, so come Friday night, you'd put on the gear and go up the pub, leave the scooters at home, have a few beers, decide who was going to drive. We used to go up a local nightclub and there was always a big mixture of people – blacks, skinheads, and all the lads from the smaller towns – so there was always a lot of trouble. That was just the sort of place it was. If we got bored, we'd go to a disco in a smaller town and they'd immediately see you as alien because you were dressed differently – short hair, suits, Sta-press, whatever – while they were just average boys about town. You'd ask the DJ to play some reggae – they'd always have Al Capone, Israelites – and you'd start dancing and talking to some of the girls, and you could guarantee the local lads would come over. You were different, coming into their club, dancing to strange records, chatting their girls up, so it would always kick off. Then, it was just a laugh, great fun. You'd always end up having a punch up. Everything would go flying, chairs and tables and whatever, you against them, a big divide down the middle. Because you were dressed differently, you attracted trouble and people thought you were looking for it."

"There's nothing like being in a gang," recalls Lee Thompson, who would go on to find fame and fortune with Madness, a band who were at least partly responsible for the return of ska in the late Seventies and the reason behind a new generation of school kids shaving their heads and lacing up a pair of boots. "I first saw skinheads in about '68 and I thought, I like that. There was a pair of flares laid out in front of me and a pair of Doctor Martens and for some reason the Doctor Martens appealed to me more than the pair of flares. Plus, the people I knocked about with were that way inclined – shaved heads, jackets… it was a good year for fashion. We used to knock about Parliament Hill Fields and we were called the Highgate. The leader of the gang was Dave Nash and the next in line was a chap called Dennis and they must have only been five foot three, but they looked eight feet tall. We used to do stupid things like smashing windows and that. There was a bowling green next to us where old people used to enjoy their Sunday afternoons and, one day, we went over there with our steel combs and carved our names in the bowling pitch. They had to take the whole thing up and re-lay it."

Britain has given birth to countless youth cults since the Second World War, but few come close to challenging skinheads who represent the greatest of them all. And that's particularly true of the original skinhead era. At the time, communities were being demolished to make way for high-rise flats and jobs were being replaced by machines, and somehow the skinhead cult, with its style, passion, power, defiance and aggression, seemed to be the perfect celebration of working class pride. Skinheads worked hard and played hard. They went cap in hand to nobody. They were smart, clean and sussed. To be a skinhead was to join in the celebration, it was about standing together with your mates, it was about being somebody in a world of nobodies. At face value, it was just another fad, but its roots were so powerful and meant so much to those involved in it that the cult has stood the test of time for nearly 30 years now.

"1970, on holiday somewhere down south, I first saw a gang of skinheads running riot around this seaside town," remembers Nidge Miller, later of Oi! band, Blitz. "A week later, I had my head shaved, got my boots, my braces, and a shirt. Almost everyone was a skinhead really. Back then, you were a skinhead or nothing."

No Mean City

The importance of fanzines for street culture can never be overstated. The vast majority never last more than a few poorly photocopied issues, but each and every one plays its part in spreading the gospel far and wide. Whether they have only a few readers or a few thousand, it doesn't really matter, just as long as they let people know about gigs, record releases, new bands and so on.

For my money, the skinhead fanzine that deserves to go down in history as the dog's bollocks is Hard As Nails. It wasn't the biggest selling skinzine of all time and it wasn't the most professionally produced one there has ever been either. It wasn't even always particularly brilliant – as I'm sure Paul and Ian, the two Canvey Island skinheads who produced it, would be the first to tell you. In fact, today, there are thousands of skinheads who have never even heard of it, but without this little A5 size fanzine, the skinhead cult would not be what it is today.

When it first appeared towards the end of 1983, the skinhead cult was in a sorry state, if the truth be told. 2 Tone was long gone and the glory days of Oi! had more or less passed too. A lot of the top skinheads from the last few years had either hung up their boots or turned casual to pursue a career in football violence. Standards had hit an all-time low for what is the proudest of all youth cults, and there was a real danger that the cult would drown in a sea of glue-sniffing bald punks who could hardly get any further away from the true traditions and values of the skinhead cult.

That wasn't to say that all skinheads had given up caring about style and music. Pockets of resistance existed in towns and cities like Cardiff, Dublin, Newcastle, Plymouth, and Glasgow. What Hard As Nails did was provide a base camp for these and other skins, and basically offered an alternative vision of what the cult was truly about.

After the demise of Hard As Nails, Glasgow seemed to become the focus for the sussed skinhead way of life, largely thanks to the efforts of the Glasgow Spy Kids skinhead crew. Not only were three fanzines based in Glasgow at the time – McGinn's Bovver Boot, Big Ewan's Spy Kids, and my own Zoot! – but there were regular reggae and soul dances, and the city had a real buzz about it if you were a skinhead, a rudy, mod, scooterist or of similar persuasion.

"The Spy Kids came about through drinking," explains McGinn, one of the leading lights on the Glasgow scene for many years, not least because of his patter. A natural storyteller if ever there was one. "It was a thing going about at the time – the Hard As Nails fanzine, the sussed skin – and that sort of appealed to us. So we got our own mob together, decided on a name and a focus, and we trooped off to get the tattoo. It was just like-minded people. It was about reggae, being smart, and away from the glue and the boneheads. Sometimes, we thought we were fighting for the real side of skinhead, but most of the time we'd fight because we'd be full of drink and it seemed like a good idea!"

Ten years after the Spy Kids started, only Big Iain is still a skinhead and he remembers the crew's roots in much the same way.

"In 1985, there were still quite a lot of skinheads in Glasgow, a lot of boneheads, but a few of us broke away and formed our own crew based on the smarter version of skinhead. We made up our own name which was basically another name for skinheads before they were actually called skinheads. We drank up the East End in a bar called the One Up, which before then was basically a mod club. We got on all right with the mods and held dances with them. We organised '69 style dances with smart dress only, same as the mod dances. We attracted quite a few skinheads from around the town and ended up with quite a decent mob into the same things – dressing in suits, Ben Sherman shirts, smart shoes instead of boots at night, and listening to reggae and soul music all night."

The Spy Kids somehow managed to bring together smartly dressed skinheads from all over the city and beyond. They crossed the sectarian divide, football teams, everything – in a bid to present a united front of skinhead style. And there was no doubting that these boys had style, with tonic suits, Sta-press, button-down shirts, highly polished boots, and so on being the order of the day. What's more, most of it was picked up for next to nothing at Paddy's Market, The Barras market, and various charity shops around the city. Working class style at working class prices.

There was a rival mob in the city called the Combat Skins, and they had close relatives in neighbouring towns like Paisley, Greenock, and Falkirk. That's not to say that all skinheads from those towns were racist (Big Ewan was himself from Paisley), but their main mobs were as far as anyone in Glasgow knew. The Combats, led by a long-time skinhead called Spearsey, were white power skins who favoured the bald punk look to that of the traditional skinhead, but they went into decline anyway as The Spy Kids grew in status, and by the end of the Eighties they had more or less disappeared from sight.

The reasons for The Spy Kids totally rejecting the white power scene were many, and are worth noting because it illustrates why where you are brought up influences your beliefs.

Scotland, and Glasgow in particular, has a long socialist tradition and there has never been a great deal of support for the right wing, except when aligned to the Protestant faith and the Ulster cause. What's more, the immigrant population in Scotland – mainly Pakistani, Chinese, Polish, and Italian – is very small and so causes less resentment than it may do in areas of a higher concentration of immigrants. In fact, it is estimated that over seven million Scots live abroad, while just over five million live at home, so, like the Irish, we should be the last ones to talk about sending foreigners home. The West coast of Scotland has its own angle on bigotry anyway based on the rivalry between Catholics and Protestants. Me, I've never understood it and have no time for it, but a surprising number of people take it very seriously indeed. The Spy Kids had no time for it either, beyond the usual football-related jibes (for those not in the know, Celtic is very much a Catholic team, while Rangers is staunchly Protestant. Partick Thistle, the city's other big club, revels in the fact that "We're nothing but a football team, so fuck your Pope and fuck your Queen!").

In the Sixties, Glasgow boasted more hard mods than any other city in Britain. In early 1969, just as hard mod finally gave way to the skinhead cult in the city, the singer Frankie Vaughan went to Easterhouse and announced a gang amnesty after years of increasingly serious disputes between Glasgow gangs. When mod returned in the late Seventies, it was the hard mod image that was evoked, just as it was in East London with the Glory Boys. United by both style and music, the Glasgow mods were a prominent feature of city street life right into the Eighties.

In 1982, The Exploited and Infa Riot played at a Gathering Of The Clans gig at the Apollo, but before and afterwards, punks had to run the gauntlet of a marauding army of mods who didn't take kindly to the studs and leather invasion.

Those who had been mods in the late Seventies and early Eighties were already arch-rivals of the Combat Skins. The mods would spend many a Saturday roaming around the city centre looking for bikers and skinheads to bash, and, in the early Eighties, that included smartly dressed skins too. It was a case of shoot first, and ask questions later really.

That said, the likes of Quinny, who later became a Spy Kid, had a better idea of what the original skinhead cult was all about than most of the skins in the town at the time.

"For me coming from the mod thing, I knew that the roots of skinheads lay with reggae. I was about 18 when I saw characters like McGinn about the town and thought they looked quite sharp-looking. And being a mod, I wanted to look sharp."

The funny thing was, the very characters Quinny was seeing around the town had initially become involved in the skinhead cult without having a clue about its origins.

"Before becoming a skinhead, I always liked a bit of punk rock, but I never had a mohican or any of that silly nonsense," McGinn recalls. "I became a skinhead when I was 'round about 12, 13. The look of it attracted me. There was mods and skinheads, and mod seemed a bit expensive dress-wise, so that's why I became a skin. Big boots, cropped hair, a working class look. Young, aggressive, and I thought, that's for me. The first time I had a crop, I felt tremendous. A bovver boy. I thought, fucking great, look at the state of me! Head shaved, big boots and that. The hard man thing, especially in Glasgow, where it's a sort of cliché. All the guys at school that liked heavy metal were the rich kids, the horrible spotty loner types. They always seemed to get picked on and beaten up – which is basically acceptable..."

McGinn had first seen skinheads at a Sham 69 matinee concert in the city, and was hooked by the look. The music he liked stayed firmly in the street punk world, and 2 Tone never really got a look in until its glory days had passed. The same went for others like Big Iain who loved Oi! and street punk, and who didn't actually believe 2 Tone had anything to do with being a skinhead.

"Now, all I listen to is Sixties and early Seventies Jamaican reggae and American soul. The first bands that really got me into skinhead were The Cockney Rejects and The Angelic Upstarts, The 4 Skins, The Business, and that. Then, I started to listen to what original skinhead music was – reggae and soul. You start getting into it because you feel you should be getting into it, and then once you have an ear for it, it sounds amazing."

Nowadays, anyone wanting to become a skinhead has it really easy – the music, the clothes, and how many times to shake your dick after having a piss have all been documented in books and fanzines for all to see. But, back then, you had loads of kids running about who didn't have a clue what skinhead was about. The late Seventies really were naive times in so many ways.

McGinn again. "You hung about your own area with your mates. The only reason to come up the town was for gigs. When you were 13, 14, you did the same things – played football, messed about, loitered about at night – but you just did it with skinhead clothes on. What attracted you was the look before the music or history. Everybody thought it was just the violence thing – and that was part of the attraction as such – but when you looked back and saw a lot of things we knew nothing about, like skinhead coming from the black thing, the rude boys, that was a complete shock."

As the Eighties started to tick by, most of the kids into skinhead for the fashion traded in their boots for the next big thing. As with all cults, the die-hards stayed with it though, but had to start looking a bit further afield for like-minded individuals. You would meet skins in the street or at gigs, and find out where other skinheads were drinking, and slowly, but surely a new scene evolved. By the mid-Eighties, the surviving skinheads in and around Glasgow who would become Spy Kids had discovered more about the origins of the cult, mainly through the likes of a skinhead called Keg whose older brothers had been skinheads for much of the Seventies, and through Nick Knight's Skinhead book and Hard As Nails. In fact Nick Knight's Skinhead book was bought not so much for the photos (and certainly not for the sociological bullshit that bordered on the apologetic), but for Jim Ferguson's Fashion Notebook chapter.

"More skinheads began to follow the styles in that book," says Big Iain, "and that leads you back to where the styles came from and where the actual skinhead scene came from. By '84-'85, Hard As Nails fanzine started coming out and it was totally based on the style of the original skinheads. When people started reading that, they saw where the cult really came from – out of the mod scene – and how it was based on a smart, clean, hard look."

By looking back at the cult's roots, a whole range of largely forgotten sounds was just waiting to be discovered too, and more and more of the local skinheads began to devote their energies to skinhead reggae, soul, and Jamaican ska. This love of black music was never going to allow much room for white power, and this – together with the different styles of dress – created a split that became a chasm between the two types of skinheads in the city. You were either with the Combats or with the Spy Kids – drinking with both was out of the question.

Glasgow was also home to a large scooter scene at the time, and this was dominated by the Globetrotter SC. It was truly amazing that such an array of outcasts and general misfits ever found each other in a city the size of Glasgow, but the common bond for the Globies was of course a love of scooters. If they had been born in California in a different decade, there's no doubt that the Globetrotters would have been a biker gang to list alongside the legendary Hell's Angels, Satan's Slaves, and Coffin Cheaters. As things turned out, they chose to ride Vespas and Lammys rather than Triumphs and Harleys, but they could have been riding push bikes and they would have still been one per centers.

Trouble was never far away, and they regularly got the jail at the weekend. The media always goes overboard about skinhead violence, but the real nutters in the Globetrotters weren't the few who also happened to be skins. Rambo's party trick was to sit up on a ledge so that he could piss on those unfortunate enough to be sitting around the tables immediately below him. Some poor bastard would be sipping his beer, listening to the music, and would suddenly feel this warm liquid trickling down the back of his neck. And he'd turn around to find Rambo relieving himself. Funniest thing of all, people did nothing about it because it just wasn't clever to mix it with the likes of Rambo.

The 1987 Scottish Scooter Custom Show, which was held at a sports centre in Livingston, was a typical day out for the Globetrotters. There was only around a dozen of them, crammed into the back of a hired transit van with a dodgy mile gauge that was to claim that it had been around the world three times in the space of 12 hours. Anyway, the Clyde Panthers SC from Greenock had taken a coachload through, and a large number of them were white power skinheads who formed the hardcore following for Greenock White Noise band, New Dawn.

The Globies went expecting aggro – the van was tooled up better than the local ironmonger's – and things kicked off as soon as Madness' The Prince was played at the evening disco. Exception was taken to a handful of boneheads sieg heiling, Popeye ran over and smacked one in the mouth, and the dancefloor suddenly became a war zone. The bouncers – big bodybuilding bastards who trained at the sports centre – started throwing people out, and although outnumbered inside the centre, things were now far more even for the Globetrotters outside. The end result was the boneheads getting a good hiding outside, and the five or so Globies left inside needing a police escort out of the building amid threats that they were going to get their throats' cut by the baldies who hadn't been thrown out, but had seen their mates carted off in ambulances.

Like The Spy Kids, The Globetrotters came from all over Glasgow, unusual for a city that is traditionally very gang orientated along the lines of territory. More surprisingly still, they had three Pakistanis – Rikki, Joe, and Big Baz – in the club, and so it was difficult to be racist on the Glasgow scooter scene without crossing The Globetrotters.

Rikki went on to open a scooter shop called Zoot Scootz, and when Nazis and the like came in for scooter parts, they would always take any racist badges off their flight jackets so as not to offend him. Rikki actually had a scooter called The Black Gestapo, a name taken from a New York black street gang who had appeared in a cheap video he'd seen. The scooter was a chopper and came complete with a petrol tank with the name Black Gestapo and a swastika painted on it. Quite often he'd arrive at the rallies with his helmet on (painted in the Globetrotters' red, white and blue colours) and people would just assume he was a Nazi – until of course he took his lid off.

Anyway, The Glasgow Herald newspaper did a big feature on racism in Glasgow at the time, and it included a photo of Rikki's scooter as proof of the racist menace at large in an area with a high Asian population. The cutting was pinned to his shop wall and he was quite proud of it.

"I used to go to the scooter rallies with all the other boys and you always used to see Nazis. You'd get trouble all the time, but if you could handle yourself, you'd be okay. Our club, the Glasgow Globetrotters, always used to stick together. We had three Asians, the rest were white, skinheads and that, but we were like a family. It's only if you are on your own that they'd start on you. A couple of times, you'd get guys calling you names, and you'd say, 'Come on then, you and me, a square go', and they couldn't believe it. They'd think, what's this Asian guy doing, wanting to fight me?"

Rikki came from Bradford and lives there now where he runs a kebab shop. He got involved in the skinhead scene down there in the late Seventies and early Eighties, thanks to his love of 2 Tone and scooters.

"My family didn't like it at all. I got kicked out of the house a few times because they wanted me to change, but all my mates were into ska and I just followed them. It was really hard for them to understand because no other Asians were into it, but they accepted it in the end. You get people who say all skinheads are Nazis, but that's not the case. It's hard for someone walking down the street. They see a skinhead and think he's a Nazi, but a lot of my friends are skinheads and you get to know there are two types of skinheads. Any time I needed a hand from them, they'd help me out."

The Spy Kids and Globetrotters had much in common and spent most weekends together in and around the One Up Bar on Kent Street, a pub-cum-cafe that has now sadly closed. It was the place to be at the weekend for mods, skins and scooterists, and was rarely used by anyone else. When there was no soul or reggae dances to go to, everyone would end up at one of the alternative music clubs in the town.

"We used to go to different clubs like Vamps, and one night, four or five guys sieg heiled me as I walked past them," says Rikki. "My mates were with me, but at the time I was walking about on my own. I figured out who they were, how many, and what have you. Then I gave my mates a shout, and the next time they 'sieged' they didn't get the 'heil' out. Another time, we were at a gig and this skinhead kept looking at me, really giving me some vibes. So anyway, a fight starts off, and we're all thrown out. I saw this skinhead outside, went up to him, and all of a sudden his face changed. He had all these tattoos on his face – Made In Britain, Made In Scotland, what have you – but before I'd even hit him he started crying. I just beat him up and that was it really. They're just like any other guy. Get them by themselves and they're nothing."

The One Up Bar played host to regular reggae and soul dances and they attracted skinheads from other parts of Scotland, as well as from south of the border. Paul from Hard As Nails came up, as did skinheads from Leeds, Newcastle, Cardiff, Plymouth, and elsewhere. Only once did a muggy crew show up, and to this day nobody knows exactly where they came from. The only clue was that most of them sported Bristol Rovers National Front t-shirts, but whether they actually came from Bristol or not, nobody bothered to find out. Things didn't start too well for them when one of their numbers presented the DJ with a Skrewdriver single and asked him to play it. The DJ took it, looked at it, snapped it in half, and handed it back before getting back to playing some northern soul. They ended up getting kicked up and down outside the pub as the dance came to an end, and despite regular threats from various other mobs, nobody else looking for trouble ever showed their faces at the One Up.

That is unless you count the Aberdeen Soccer Casuals. Jay Allen's Bloody Casuals book (Famedram) about his times with the ASC prior to him and the other top boys being arrested and imprisoned for football hooliganism tells a story about how they ran the mods and skinheads down a side street as they fought Celtic fans along the London Road on their way to Parkhead, home of Celtic. Jay talks about the mods and skinheads running, a few scooters getting kicked over and then he gets back to the battle proper along the London Road.

As you'll know all good stories have at least two sides. I wasn't there that afternoon, but I'm reliably informed that later that same day, on the junction of Argyle Street and Union Street, around 100 Glasgow mods stumbled upon some of the Aberdeen casuals as they were heading home and gave a few of them a good hiding. In fact Big Stevie, who later became a Spy Kid, chased one of the casuals across the road and both ran straight into the path of an oncoming car. Ouch.

A few years later, Celtic played Aberdeen in the Scottish Cup final and while walking down Union Street, three or four Glasgow skins crossed the path of around 100 Aberdeen casuals who were marching towards Central Station, chanting, "Nobody kicks the fuck out of you like an Aberdeen soccer crew!" Fortunately enough, skinheads were of no interest to them that day and the skins made it to the nearest pub (as you do) in one piece.

Another favourite activity of The Spy Kids was buying cheap wine and beer, and drinking it at the bandstand down by the River Clyde. Weather permitting, of course. When money was tight and the summer nights long, this was a popular option as off-licence prices are far cheaper than bar prices, especially when you're drinking Buckfast and El-D, and not pints of Tennents. That said, a lot of the beer pulled at the One Up was never actually paid for anyway, no doubt a major influence on the owner eventually closing the place down. A succession of pubs followed, the best probably being downstairs at the Ingram since the skinheads had it to themselves, but that's now been turned into a wine bar.

Politics as such never played any real part in the Spy Kids' life. A couple of the boys were interested in politics, but beyond bashing Nazis, it's fair to say that most of them were more interested in style, music, sex, and getting pissed. In fact, white power skinheads were more a target because they were "muggy bonehead bastards" and because of the scruffy way a lot of them dressed rather than because of their politics. One of the Spy Kids, Big Ewan, had actually been a Nazi skinhead before seeing the light, and he had 'Skrewdriver' tattooed on his arm. Obviously that didn't go with being a Spy Kid and so he got 'Are Bastards' inked underneath.

Ewan was a decent bloke and this story isn't told to make him look stupid or anything. It's just to show that people do change, people do make mistakes, and that life is far more complicated than some try to make out.

"Politics shouldn't have anything to do with the cult and it really hasn't," explains Big Iain. "The media tries to keep it alive that skinheads are a right-wing group that cause trouble, but just about every skinhead I know has nothing to do with politics. There are still some groups who call themselves skinheads, but to me, a baldy napper and a black pilot jacket do not make you a skinhead. Everyone has got their own politics. Mine are what I'd call working class politics and I vote Labour, but I'm not extreme in any way. I take people as I find them. It's the media that has built politics up to be a skinhead thing."

McGinn was perhaps the most staunchly anti-fascist Spy Kid for political reasons, and the fact that he was very much a prominent figure in the crew and responsible for Bovver Boot, arranging dances and the like, meant others naturally supported him. That, after all, is what mates are for. But even

McGinn reckons that politics should never have had a place in the cult, and despite the Spy Kids' reputation for being an anti-Nazi crew, politics was never an issue or even talked about. A few of them were traditional Labour voters, like Big Iain, but that's as far as it went. Any fights against the Nazis had as much to do with defending the true traditions of the skinhead cult as it did politics. In fact, if Nazis had latched on to goths in a big way instead of skinheads, most of the Spy Kids wouldn't have given them a second thought.

It's also interesting to note that no Spy Kid felt the need to actively support SHARP (Skinheads Against Racial Prejudice) when it was imported to these shores from the USA. As far as they were concerned, there was only one true breed of skinhead anyway. The old breed. And you didn't need any labels or tags beyond that of skinhead.

When The Redskins came to town, everyone trooped along, as much to noise up the largely student audience as to hear what was a superb band. Nobody was particularly interested in the SWP preachers who got up on stage between bands to talk about the forthcoming revolution, but The Redskins as a band were inspirational, just as Dexy's Midnight Runners, The Specials, The Jam, and others had been before them. Not necessarily in a party political sense, not for the Spy Kids anyway, but in a get up off your backsides and get out there and do something for yourself sense.

"We got up to the usual," says McGinn. "It's always classed as skinhead – going to football, drinking, fighting – but it's really just a youth thing. We'd put on dances, try and create something, and give it some momentum. It was just a good time, a good carry on with good mates."

There's no doubt that as a skinhead in Glasgow in the late Eighties, you really did think you were part of something special, something important. It was all about pride – pride in yourself, pride in the skinhead cult, pride in your way of life. A last stand for traditional working class values as has been made by the original skinheads twenty years beforehand, and a genuine belief that you were taking the cult back to its rightful roots. The Spy Kids' Spirit Of '69 motto seemed to capture the mood perfectly.

Gig-wise, Glasgow was never going to have the pulling power of London. In fact, rather than travel four hundred miles north from the Big Smoke, it's easier for London bands to play over in Europe, and more profitable too. That left the Spy Kids to make regular pilgrimages south to the International Ska Festivals, and to catch up with the top bands of the day – The Potato 5, The Deltones, The Trojans, and Maroon Town. The more lightweight and less authentic ska sound that became increasingly popular as the Eighties gave way to the Nineties never went down as well in Glasgow circles.

The city did have one of the finest revival ska bands of the time though in the shape of Capone & The Bullets. Their phobia about recording studios was the main reason their local fame didn't translate into national fortune, but nobody in Glasgow was complaining as, live, they were up there with the best of them. After being invited to play at a dance down at the One Up, they quickly picked up a skinhead following which turned up at virtually every gig they played. They once played a gig just off Charing Cross and afterwards the Speaker's Corner pub was literally full of 100 plus skinheads.

Perhaps, the band's best night in Glasgow though was when Laurel Aitken paid his first visit to the city in 1987 and Capone & The Bullets played their own set before providing the backing for Laurel at a show at Hollywood Studios down by the Broomielaw. It was one of those gigs where the atmosphere was truly electric – Laurel ended the gig dancing on tables – and it's a gig that's still talked about as if it happened yesterday. The following summer, a series of gigs at Rooftops on Sauchiehall Street brought the likes of the Potato 5, The Toasters, The Riffs, The Loafers, and The Hotknives to the city and some more good times were had. There was also another ska band in the city called The Banditos which was started by Big Terry from Maryhill and some young skinheads who appeared about the same time as the underground ska revival was in full swing. Some good times were had at their shows too, but like all good things, it couldn't last forever.

"Skinhead is basically a teenage thing," argues McGinn. "That's when you feel you can really excel at it. But when you're 25-26, I started feeling a bit self-conscious walking about with big boots and a shaved head. It's basically a youth thing. The Spy Kids was a focus, but it gradually fell away, and there was hardly anything happening, no bands, nowhere to go, dwindling numbers, and it became kind of boring. You get to a certain age and take on other responsibilities – family and that. You always carry a torch for it though. It was the coolest and smartest thing to be into it. It gave you a sense of identity."

It took a while for the Spy Kids crew to disperse. People moved away, got married, had kids, joined the Paras, the usual things. But it obviously wasn't an easy thing to walk away from. Nobody knew what clothes to wear, what their friends would say, what hair style to go for.

"It was a sad day when I hung up my boots," remembers Quinny. "You feel like you're not pulling your weight and you're letting the side down."

The Spy Kids may have gone, but the skinhead faith lives on in Glasgow, thanks to Big Iain and a new generation of skinheads largely centred around the Spectrum scooter club. Everyone agrees it's nowhere near as good as it once was, and the biggest worry is the total lack of new blood entering the scene, but at least Glasgow still boasts a small firm of boots and braces merchants.

"It sounds a bit clichéd, but skinhead is a way of life," says Big Iain. "Now, you don't even think of yourself as a skinhead, it's just the way you live. When I was 17, I thought I'd be a skinhead until I was about 19, but by the time you're 19, you're not even thinking about packing it in. You're moving on, progressing through the cult. Why should I pack it in? It'd leave a big void in my life. It's all you know. It's still brilliant when you go away for the weekend, to a scooter rally or wherever, and there's 100-150 skinheads dancing away to reggae. It's still the best feeling in the world."

Here Comes Johnny Reggae

"The shirts you wear are a distinct style," says Big Iain with obvious pride as he talks you through his wardrobe. "They're button down, late Sixties-Seventies style, big collar, quite hard to find now. Ben Sherman, Brutus, Arnold Palmer, Jaytex or a similar style to them. Your jeans are usually Levi's or Wrangler, nothing else, and with Levi's preferably big E which are very hard to come by. They've got white stitching on the inside and there's a capital E on the Levi's badge (as in 'LEVI'S') - most Levi's today have the small E (as in 'Levi's'). Sta-press, smart trousers if you're not wearing a suit, again Levi's, Fred Perry. You don't really get them anymore – it's all early and late Seventies.

"Shoes are brogues or loafers. Some people wear Doc shoes which you can get away with. You can get away with any kind of boots as long as they're not silly looking. Up here, most people wear red Docs. The colour of laces doesn't mean anything no matter what people might tell you. They mean different things in different areas, but basically they don't mean a thing. A lot of people wear football colours. I wear red and white laces because I support Airdrieonians. Steel toe cap boots still go with your Levi's two piece. The Fred Perry is eternal, preferably an old type with the stripes and that on, the bigger the collar the better, the more buttons the smarter. Jackets can range from Levi's, Wrangler, golf jackets, Harringtons. Dressier jacket – crombie, sheepskin. Suits, three, four, five button even, ticket pockets – the more the better – pure Sixties, early Seventies style."

According to the style gurus, skinheads have long since passed their sell by date. We're out of step with what the glossy magazines, television programmes, and High Street shops are doing their best to sell, sell, sell. They want to tell you what's hot and what's not because that's how they make their money. Good luck to them too, but you are as likely to find true style in shops as you are money on trees. Because what these people are selling isn't style at all. It's fashion. Written big and bold in capital letters. F-A-S-H-I-O-N.

It's very easy to be taken in by it all. Attractive models pouting and strutting their way along the catwalks, or posing so sincerely for yet another photo spread. Tailor-made clothes to make your mouth water – as long as you can swallow the price tags that is. Surprising though it may be, not everyone can afford to spend £40 on a pair of socks. While the lucky few can sit in wine bars wearing suits by Hans Van Kooten, dresses by Ann Demeulemeester, and smiles by Persil Automatic, the rest of us are left to fight over the mass produced fodder that fills your High Street shops.

You know what you are supposed to look like, but unless you have the money to match your appetite – unlucky. Scratch away at the gloss coating though, and you reveal the total emptiness of fashion. Not that it bothers the fashion industry, mind you. They just come along and paint a new coat of gloss – a different colour for a different fashion. A new range for Autumn, Spring, what have you. And people fall for it time after time. Buy, buy, buy.

Fortunately, there's hope for us all because at the cutting edge of fashion is style. It doesn't come from glossy pages or the like. It comes straight from the heart. And at the top of the tree is skinhead style. Proud, hard, independent, honest, smart as fuck. All of this and more. Not bad for days like this.

As with so much of skinhead culture, the mainstream media has sought to create a myth that skinheads have no style. Watch any programme on TV that includes skinheads as characters, and time after time you'll see the same old folk devil with no brains and big boots. It's bad enough that scriptwriters get paid good money for coming up with the same old boring story lines – in the space of six months on British TV, Cracker, Between The Lines, The Bill, Casualty, and every other drama series trotted out the "racist skinhead" episode – but they should at least make an effort to accurately portray skinheads as they are.

TV skinheads are nearly always played by actors with fake Cockney accents. They invariably have tattoos on their faces, wear dirty boots, ripped jeans, glue stained Union Jack t-shirts, and dodgy flight jackets. They look more like scarecrows than skinheads.

Skinhead style and clothing has varied over the years, but it has always been about dressing hard, dressing smart. If being a skinhead means anything, it means having pride in yourself, and that has always been reflected in our style.

Different skinheads have different ideas about how they should dress. Without doubt, the smartest look is the traditional one, handed down to future generations by the original skinheads of the late 1960s and early Seventies. In those days, people dressed more formally anyway, and with the skinhead cult drawing heavily on the mods who went before them, it is little wonder that they developed the most sussed street dress around. If you talk to anyone who wore skinhead fashion in the late Sixties and early Seventies, the attention to detail, the clothes to be seen in, and the variety available, comes flooding back as if you were only talking about yesterday.

Chrissy Boy Foreman - "I remember seeing someone at school wearing a Harrington, and I thought, what's that – it looks really good. When they first came out, they were black and blue, but then they started to diversify and you got Prince Of Wales checked ones and they looked really smart. At school, you had to wear white shirts, and a white Ben Sherman looked so much better than those little nylon ones – which is what I had! And things like black Sta-press looked much better than the old John Lewis naff black trousers, and it was the same for brogues, things like that."

Gaz Mayall - "I was walking down the street when I was about nine years old, and I saw one of my best friends coming the other way, and I didn't know what a skinhead was, but the kid with him looked like the mafia – he had on a shiny suit, his shades, and highly polished loafers. Impeccable dress, the smartest guy in the whole street."

Stuart from Bridlington - "It was really easy to pick up birds with a nice scooter and smart clothes. The birds were interested in you because you were different and you dressed nice. I used to spend hours and hours making sure my boots were shiny. You could use them as mirrors nearly. My clothes were always pressed. We didn't have a lot of money then because we were pretty poor, so you'd wash your clothes in the sink so they were clean for when you went out. Skinheads took a lot of pride in how they looked."

The skinhead haircut itself has been described as half-soldier, half-convict, and most skins are happy enough to go along with that. But what most commentators miss is the fact that a shaved head, particularly with a thin shaved parting down the left side to the crown, looks incredibly smart. Add a pair of sideburns – all the rage at the time – and you definitely looked the business.

"You felt confident with yourself," says Steve Goodman about the first time he shaved his head, "but there were a lot of piss-takers at the time. Like that playground chant, 'Skinhead, skinhead, over there, what's it like to have no hair?'"

"I was up the Hope & Anchor with John Hassler, one time drummer and one time manager with Madness," says Lee Thompson, "and it was when we first got our new little gang together – Carl and Suggs and Si and everyone – and we used to get our hair cut down at Pratt Street by a bloke called George. It was like 50p to have your head shaved, so I said to John, 'Get your hair cut, get that mop on your head shaved off, and I will pay for that haircut'. And he went and got it done and his ears were out here and his lips were out there and he looked a right pratt. I never even paid him for it. John – it's in the post!"

In the late Sixties and early Seventies, skinheads would dress for the occasion. If it was hanging about on street corners, a few pints on the way home from work, or standing on the football terraces, boots and jeans would usually be worn. Boots were not only the perfect weapon, particularly if they had steel toe caps, but they also emphasised the skinhead's working class traditions. Unlike hippies and other middle class drop outs, skinheads – like their fathers – believed in working for their money, and a working man's boots left nobody in any doubt about that.

"Doctor Martens underneath a size 4 were half sole and it was really embarrassing," recalls Lee Thompson, who was a size 3 at the time. "I think they lasted me a month before Dave Nash, who was a size 8, said, 'You don't want to wear those, you want to wear these.' So I put them on and they were like four inches too big for me! I remember packing them with newspaper, and walking about wearing these massive big boots, but at least they had a full sole."

Jeans too were very practical, but would always be clean, pressed, and a recognised brand – Levi's, Wrangler and Lee being favourites. Some skins even ironed creases in them, just as you would your best suit, a tradition that still lives on today in some skinhead circles. Other skins might chose to wear a pair of Sta-press trousers, so-called because they never needed to see an iron (in theory anyway). Levi's made the best Sta-press money could buy – and their white ones were never equalled.

T-shirts and Fred Perry polo shirts were on regular display, but most skinheads still preferred to wear shirts. Collarless shirts, often called union shirts, were popular for a time, but American style button down shirts were the really big sellers. Again, if you could afford brand names like Ben Sherman, Brutus, and Jaytex, all the better.

If you were going to a gig or out on the pull, chances were you'd be wearing a suit. Tonic, mohair, plain, Prince of Wales check, whatever happened to be the flavour of the month at the time.

"The original skinheads evolved out of mods," says Brian Kelson. "The clothes, the Sta-press, the brogues, the suits, meant skinheads were always smartly dressed in the evening. During the daytime, it was jeans and boots."

For skinhead girls, the fashions were much the same, although the haircut was almost always a feathercut and very rarely shaved like the boys.

"It's about looking smart", says Jacquel, a skingirl who originally dressed in the more severe punk-influenced skinhead way, but who now dresses as originally as possible. "I've got a couple of three quarter length suits made out of good quality two tone cloth, old style shirts which are now hard to come by, Levi's jeans, Levi's and Wrangler jackets. It's all quite particular, but above all it's smart. My hair's longer now and more in an original style too."

Most people assume that skinhead more or less died out, and was then brought back to life by street punk bands like Cock Sparrer, Menace, Slaughter & The Dogs, and Sham 69, with Jimmy Pursey's now famous "Skinheads are back!" battle cry. It's true that by the summer of '78, there was a mass skinhead revival happening, but well before the likes of Sham, skinheads were already making a comeback.

"Around the end of '75 and the start of '76, we were getting pissed off with things in general," says Dite, who first became a skinhead in 1970 and by the mid-Seventies was languishing in the post-glam post-bootboy era. "Most music was boring and crap, and even old favourites like Slade were losing it. Good gear was getting harder to find and the skinhead days seemed like a lifetime away. Our unofficial leader, Dale Watson, was true to the faith and remained a skinhead throughout.

"We were still most definitely a bootboy crew and still wore DMs, the most important part of the bootboy uniform. There were others in different towns who called themselves bootboys, but they didn't look the part in desert boots, Adidas trainers, flared Levi's, and leather jackets. One day, myself and a mate Jake were discussing such matters and decided to go back to our roots. Despite the threats from our girlfriends ('get a skinhead and I'll chuck you'), we became skins again. And the girls loved it.

"Now there were three skinheads in Montrose and for all we knew Scotland, although we didn't want to believe that. Before we knew it, all our mates had followed suit, and we were a skinhead crew again. The search was on for original gear, but it was largely in vain. So our look consisted mainly of Wrangler and Levi's jackets, Harringtons, braces, t-shirts, Skinners, parallels, granddad or union shirts which were popular at the time, and 10-hole Air Wair. What really mattered was the spirit was there."

All of this was happening in 1976, and before punk had arrived, let alone Sham 69. What's more, within a month of Dite and his friends turning skinhead, nearly every kid in Montrose had shaved their head too, giving rise to most probably the biggest skinhead crew of that time. In the Midlands and the north of England, most kids had followed the fashions from skinhead to suedehead to crombie boy to bootboy and then into northern soul. Fashion was at a post-war low and then punk arrived, a look that a lot of people who had been original skinheads just could not relate to. Punks were just a variation on hippies and bikers.

"I can actually remember there being three or four of us in a mate's car and we were talking about this," recalls Brian Kelson, looking back to 1976, "and we said we had to do something, be something, and we all agreed the best thing we'd ever been into was skinheads. So that was it. We went out the next day to a shop in Wolverhampton, where we knew they used to sell the gear years ago, and he had a load of tonic suits left so we bought them up. You could still get loafers in the shops, and that was it. We were skinheads again. It seemed ideal – it was a smart look and a tough look so you had the best of both worlds."

Brian Kelson also used to meet up with skinheads on his trips down to watch Chelsea at Stamford Bridge around this time. Even the first skins to follow Sham 69 were skinheads who'd stayed true to the cult throughout the Seventies. It wasn't even necessarily a love of punk that attracted them – it was either disco or punk at the time, and most nightclubs wouldn't let skinheads in so punk it was.

In London, just like in isolated cases elsewhere, some people had stayed skinheads throughout the Seventies. Gary Hitchcock, later to be well known in Oi! circles as the manager of The 4 Skins, appeared in Sounds in 1980, talking about the lead up to the skinhead revival. "I'd caught the end of skinheads when I was at school and I just loved everything about it, what it stood for. But it died down and everyone got into Budgie gear and that. But I always said if it ever came back, I'd be a skin again. In 1976, I saw a skinhead so I went and had a crop too."

After talking about Sham and the way Pursey had sold out, he went on to describe Skrewdriver as the first real skinhead band.

"We met Ian Stuart at a Sham gig at the Roxy in '77. He told us about Skrewdriver, said they weren't like Sham, that they were skins, so we spread the word about, and there was a massive turn-out. Down at the Vortex it was. We never knew there were so many skinheads around and they were all geezers. No one looked under 25, and they played all the skinhead reggae stuff that we hadn't heard in years."

Few people today would believe that skinhead reggae could be played at a Skrewdriver gig, but back then they had no political affiliations. In fact, Skrewdriver had been long haired punks just a few short months before, and were the only street punk band to shave their heads and actively court a mainly skinhead following at the time. Not that all skinheads were impressed by Skrewdriver even then.

"All Skrewed Up was crap anyway," said Dite of their debut album on Chiswick, "and press release photos at the time made them look like a bunch of scruffs."

By March 1978, Ian Stuart was writing to NME, saying, "Skrewdriver is no longer a skinhead band due to the violence at our gigs." London, in particular, was plagued by violence at gigs, and Skrewdriver obviously didn't want to inherit Sham 69's reputation for attracting aggro to gigs. Throughout that year, people were writing to the music newspapers, either complaining about skinhead gig violence, or defending skinheads, and it's interesting to note that a number of letters were sent in by skinheads who had been around since 1969.

Few seemed impressed by the new breed of skinheads. A handful of original London skinheads, who claimed to have followed Sham from the beginning when they were the only skins in the audience, said, "We've noticed that all the poseurs down the King's Road have now turned skinhead... and we're sick to the back teeth of you lot cashing in on what we had." Another original skinhead, who simply signed his letter, 'a Nottingham Forest fan' (meaning that at least one skinhead from Nottingham kept the torch burning through the dark years too) said, "So the 'true' skins support the NF eh? Bollocks! I've been a skinhead since 1969 and we hadn't even heard of the National Front then."

The influence of punk and the scarcity of traditional skinhead wear meant that the new breed of skin rarely came up to the standards of dress set just seven or eight years before. Even the music of bands like Sham and Menace was a world away from the original skinhead sounds of soul and reggae.

"The music was just like rock music," says Brian Kelson, who saw punks as a variation of hippies and bikers, "and the clothes were just so scruffy and ill-fitting. The jeans would be skin tight and too short with great big boots, and the hair was shaven right off. They'd be taking drugs and sniffing glue, and you wouldn't have caught an original skinhead doing that – it was degrading. You were a working class bloke, proud of this great nation, and you wouldn't be seen dossing like a hippy. The public saw them as dirty, scruffy, bald-headed drug takers – short-haired hippies really. To be brought up with such strong ideals about the movement and to see it taken over like that was worse than anything."

"When I first turned skinhead, all the old skinheads were giving me their clothes and I had some real class gear at the time," recalls Steve Goodman. "When you were going through '77 you couldn't get sod all. It'd be army lightweights, Harrington jacket, Fred Perry shirt. Those were the things you could pick up. Then later, when it kicked off with 2 Tone and what have you, you had a lot of gear come out labelled as mod wear, but it was just as much skinhead wear."

During the 2 Tone era, it was often difficult to tell skinheads from mods and rude boys – just as it would have been in the late Sixties. With the mod and ska revivals overlapping each other and catching the early days of Oi!, clothes manufacturers once again started to mass produce skinhead clothes. Markets in particular were full of cheap imitation crombies, Sta-press trousers and pork pie hats.

"When I was younger, I had big ideals about what everyone else should wear or shouldn't wear, but I suppose I've worn some things in my time!" adds Brian Kelson. "When I got older, I got a bit snobbish, especially with all the punk skins, and I used to dress up to be better than them, get one over them, and I got to looking down on other skinheads because they weren't dressing up to standard. But you have to realise they were just buying what they could buy. It seemed like as the Eighties went on, a lot more skinheads started dressing to the original style – which was really good. Even punk skins and the National Front lot seemed to be dressing in the original style. But by then, I knew you couldn't buy the clothes anymore, and so had stopped looking down on people."

Today, it's not so easy finding decent clothes, particularly original skinhead clothes in good condition. 20 odd years has taken its toll on even the best made stuff, and nobody is genuinely catering for skinheads these days beyond shops like The Merc and Sherry's Fashions in the Carnaby Street area of London. You can still buy Doctor Marten boots, and everyone and his dog has a pair of Levi's 501s (same goes for MA1 flight jackets). Ben Sherman still makes shirts as do Fred Perry, but neither are the same in terms of quality or design (although Fred Perry have recently re-launched the original designs again in a somewhat belated bid to cash in on the now waning Seventies clothes revival).

For the real authentic look, you're reduced to looking through second hand shops and jumble sales. Plenty of skinheads do it though, and there is real pride in being the only skin in town with a Prince Of Wales checked Harrington or a tonic pair of original Sta-press. Another option is to get clothes tailor made, and it's often the only way you'll get what you're looking for. Skinhead girls who want a suit with a three quarter length jacket are a case in point. Despite the difficulties in finding the gear, there is a definite move among skinheads back to the original skinhead look.

"People have started dressing a lot smarter now," says Phil, a skinhead from County Durham. "When I first turned skinhead, everyone was wearing 14 holers, bleached jeans, bald head, but now it's gone back to like '69 – really smart, suits, Sta-press, originally shirts. I like it better like this. I feel more proud dressing like this because I feel it's more working class."

Skinhead gigs and dances are full of skins and skinhead girls trying to look their best. It's human nature. The birds and the bees and all that. And there's no doubting that when you are dressed in your best gear, you feel on top of the world. There's nothing wrong with that, and you can have nothing but admiration for those skinheads who do their utmost to look beyond mod smart.

"Skinhead style is a progression from mod style, an extreme version of mod," says Big Iain, just one of many skinheads who believe that the traditional style is the only genuine skinhead style. "It goes from the sublime to the ridiculous. It's very smart to the extremes of being snobbish. You get looked down on if you don't have the right size collar, your boots aren't polished enough, holes in the knees of your jeans – it just isn't tolerated. It's basically smart dress, clean shaven, neat haircut, parting in your hair. A baldy head isn't a skinhead. You're either going bald or you're a bonehead. The style is a very distinct style."

The only downside to this is that snobbery has become a part of the cult. Some skinheads who have all the proper gear tend to look down on those who don't, and they think that they're somehow better than a skinhead in boots, jeans, and a t-shirt. Not all well dressed skinheads are like that, but there has always been an element within the cult who like to look down their noses at others.

"The style was important enough for me to look like a skinhead," says Gavin Watson of his days as a skin in the late Seventies and early Eighties. "You could tell I was a skinhead, but my brother and his friend were like prima donnas really, immaculately dressed and very elitist. There's a lot of snobbery in the skinhead cult, a lot of snobbery."

Snobbery is obviously nothing new, but it's certainly more prevalent in some skinhead circles today than it has ever been. There should be no place for it in the most working class cult of them all, and nobody should be made to feel inferior just because they don't have the time, the opportunity or especially the money to look like the perfect skinhead every day of the week. It goes without saying that skinheads are a breed apart, and an elite within the world of youth cults, but there are enough divisions within the cult itself without introducing dress codes that only a self-elected few can aspire to. It's one thing trying to continue the dress traditions of the original skinheads, but those who think all skinheads should have wardrobes full of tailor-made suits and drawers full of original shirts are totally missing the point. Very few of the original skinheads had that. And as one original skinhead told me when hearing the sort of money people were paying for tailor-made suits, he would have bought a car if he'd had that sort of money back then.

Even funnier is the fact that every now and again, companies like Ben Sherman would introduce a new design of shirt that totally flopped. Skinheads didn't touch it with a bargepole, and the design was quietly dropped. But today, these very same shirts are turning up on the backs of skinheads who think that ANYTHING with the right size collar and from the original era looks great. One look in the mirror will tell them otherwise.

In many ways, the skinhead cult mimics the casuals. You don't buy clothes anymore, you buy labels. You wear Levi's instead of jeans. Ben Shermans instead of shirts. Fred Perrys instead of polo shirts. Doctor Marten's instead of boots. And so it goes on. It's not as if the clothes involved are any cheaper or any better than similar clothes, especially if you live abroad and buy imported British clothes.

"It's a bit ironic that the cult is supposed to be for the low class, working man, whatever," says Pete from New York, "and yet the clothes have become so damn expensive. You pay $40-$50 for a Fred Perry shirt! I don't have to wear this stuff, but it's the style I like so I pay the prices. To be honest with you, I don't know any other way to dress anymore."

Another problem with looking down your noses at those who aren't dressed to your liking is that younger kids who know no better are made to feel unwelcome. They don't stay skinheads for very long and so never have the opportunity to learn about skinhead style for themselves. And, the fact is, everyone has to start somewhere. Even the best dressed skinheads of today will have been looked down on as "plastics" when they first turned skinhead by the veterans of the day.

A lot of skinheads follow a similar pattern. You start off with the basic gear, don't quite look the part, but do your best. Then you see what other more experienced skins are wearing and begin to learn about true style. During this phase, everything has to be perfect. Then as you get a bit older, you relax and start wearing clothes you feel good in. They might not meet with everyone's approval (try wearing trainers with jeans instead of boots for example), but you have the self-confidence to carry it off. You've served your time and can afford to move on. And eventually you leave the cult.

This was the cycle skinheads followed for years, and it was true for music as well as clothes. You started off liking a few records, but not knowing too much about bands and other skinhead music. Then you tried to learn as much as you could, and assembled some sort of record collection for credibility's sake. All those old pop singles suddenly became "your little sister's" and everything in your collection had to be skinhead related. Then you start to listen to the odd song or two from outside the skinhead world, and so it goes on until you're down at the local nightclub, bopping away to chart hits with the best of them (mind you, chances are you're still asking the DJ if he's got anything by The 4 Skins or Prince Buster).

Today though, it's possible to jump straight in at the deep end with all the right clothes and look the part from day one. The knowledge is now widely available to do just that – you just need access to the right stuff – but whether it's done the cult any real favours is arguable.

When I first discovered Ben Shermans and bought my first one, it was an incredible feeling, and I felt I had earned it in some way by making do with a Fred Perry or two while I learned the ropes. Now, though, you see someone one week who isn't a skinhead, and the next week the same person has a shaved head and all the right gear, and somehow you bedrudge them. Inverted snobbery no doubt, and again, it really shouldn't have a place in the skinhead scene today.

Given what's available to them, the majority of skinheads today do seem to make an effort to dress smartly and traditionally, although some skinheads still think the minority could try harder.

"A lot of foreign skins have missed the point," reckons Big Iain. "There's a lot of decent American skinheads, but you see some with beards. What's that about? Skinhead's about being smart, so what's a beard got to do with anything? I'd never seen a skinhead with a beard. That's just silly. And some of the gear they wear. Like you see Italian or French skinheads with hooded track tops – that's sort of half-casual, half-skinhead. You're either a skinhead or you're not, it's as simple as that. It's all about being smart and 100% into the cult. I do know some foreign skinheads who are more into the style than even me, but a lot of others miss the point. A lot of European and American skins have picked up on the extreme right wing thing, again from watching the TV, but that's not skinhead. It's just a pile of old shit."

One problem with traditional skinhead wear is that it is a very British fashion, perfect for a British climate. It's not so ideal if you live in a very hot place. When we were filming in New York in August, a handful of skinheads were wearing shorts of various descriptions, something you wouldn't see in Britain. The first day there I wore a Ben Sherman shirt, tonic Sta-press, and boots, and the humidity was killing me (your average New Yorker must have thought I was some sort of mental retard).

So, it's inevitable that as the skinhead style travels far and wide, it will be adapted to suit the locals.

"The original spirit of skinhead stood in the face of British society as proof that the working class possessed its own identity and needed no one's approval," argues Leo, a hardcore skin from New York. "It was a statement of independence from tradition, and we in America represent that tradition with conscious pride. It means a hell of a lot more to us than just wearing the 'right' clothes, which is more than I can say for some of the traditionalist skins I've met. To them, skinhead means nothing more than meticulously emulating the identity (fashion, music, politics, etc.) of the original skinheads, and in the process they give up their own identity, which to me seems like a complete contradiction.

"When someone becomes obsessively nostalgic for the outward appearance of the original skinheads, it only proves how unauthentic and fake they really are. The original skinheads weren't a bunch of kiss-arse copy-cats. They thought, acted, and dressed for themselves. We, as the current skinheads, think, act, and dress for ourselves too. Certainly, we emulate their style in a lot of ways, but we consider it part of our style, not some dogmatic commandment etched in stone to which we must pay homage. We know our beginnings and look back on the first skinheads with great respect – our movement is based on their example, but what we're doing now and where we're going is up to us."

A lot of what Leo says rings true. Even those who follow the traditional dress tend to forget that the original skinhead style never stood still. Like its mod ancestors, it was continuously evolving. What looked the business at the start of 1969 would have looked old hat come the start of 1970. But it's equally important to remember that as the style developed, the skinhead label was no longer appropriate. And so from skinhead, other cults were born – suedehead, bootboy, crombie boy, butcher coat boy, droogs and so on. And if some skinheads today are looking to travel even further away from those roots, then maybe they should be looking for a new name too which pays respect to the past, but acknowledges the present.

Being a skinhead implies an attraction to the style. To wear clothes just because you feel obliged to does show a shallowness of character, but for thousands of working class kids, the skinhead style is the perfect expression of their identity. They haven't given up their own identity, they are simply celebrating it. That will always be more the case in Britain than anywhere else, simply because that is where the cult originated.

A lot of today's skins make do with boots, jeans, braces, and a t-shirt, either because that's what they feel happiest in or because they just don't have access to the smarter look. They are every bit a skinhead as someone decked out in tonic suit and brogues.

Clothes don't make a skinhead and never will do. Anyone can go down to London, hunt around street markets, and if they have enough money, go home with a complete wardrobe of original skinhead gear. So what? That doesn't make them a skinhead. It might make them a lucky bastard, but being a skinhead is surely all about where your heart is, not how much money you've got in your bank account. As Bucket from The Toasters says, "There's a lot of people walking around now in snazzy clothes we never had when I was a kid, but the clothes don't make the man. The ideas make the man, and the feelings make the man."

Violence In Our Minds

If you ever find yourself heading south on the A13, chances are you are either lost or on your way to Tilbury in Essex. It is very much a town at the end of the line, as the End Of The World pub down by the docks testifies, and definitely not the sort of place you want to end up on your ownsome come nightfall.

For the merchant seamen who used the town's docks, it offered the chance to go ashore and spend some money on wine, women and song. Like all ports, Tilbury had its pubs that quenched the seamen's thirst for all three, and one such establishment was the now abandoned Ship Hotel. The Sun actually voted it Britain's worst pub, thanks to its reputation for prostitution, violence, and the fact that landlords lasted about as long as a packet of Durex did.

A lot of the Ship's reputation for the place to be on a Saturday night, if you fancied a good kicking, was down to the Tilbury Trojan Skins who made it a second home between 1977 and 1984. To them, it was their territory, and anyone they didn't want to drink there didn't. Not for long anyway. And the seamen often got more than they bargained for too, returning to their ships after being beaten up and robbed of their hard earned cash, watches, and anything else of value.

Naturally enough, there have always been skinheads in a dock town like Tilbury, and one who has been around longer than most is Mick White. He was a young skin back in '69, and was joined by two younger brothers, Doghead and Little Doghead (so called because they would go with any old dog of a girl), as the skinhead cult returned in force in '77 and the early Eighties.

"Back in 1977, Tilbury Docks was a rough area and it was there that skinheads took off in a big way. I'd say we were 60 strong. Ask any self-respecting skinhead from anywhere south of the Watford Gap who were the most feared mob, and Tilbury would be mentioned on more than one or two lips."

Thanks to its partial isolation, The Tilbury Trojan Skins, and later the Tilbury Young Firm, were able to build up the sort of comradeship more often found in hardcore football firms. As it was, most of the

Tilbury skins followed London teams, especially West Ham, but if things had been different and Tilbury had been home to a professional football club, there's little doubt that they would have been up there with the ICF, the Leeds Service Crew, Chelsea's Headhunters, and Portsmouth's 6:57 crew.

As luck would have it, Tilbury boasted no such team, leaving the skinheads (who also came from nearby towns like Grays and West Thurrock) free to ruck with whoever got in their way. Football supporters, foreign seamen, teddy boys, punks, mods, glue sniffers, students, queers, mobs from other towns – the list is as long as the collective charge sheet they amassed over the years. As one of the boys, Irish, put it, "We did what we wanted to do and we didn't give a monkey's about anyone else. We enjoyed ourselves, we did what we wanted. And bollocks to everyone else."

The Tilbury Skins used to follow Sham 69, and then went on to follow the likes of The Angelic Upstarts. A large slice of the London gig action at the time took place in colleges and universities – City Of London Poly, UMIST, Central London Poly, and so on – and they were as good a place as any for the Tilbury boys to see their heroes in action, not least because they could kill two birds with one stone and bash some students at the same time.

"These gigs were nearly always full of students who we all know are almost always commies, socialists, lefties or whatever you want to call them," recalls Mick White. "Nearly every single week we used to smash the fuckers as they really got on our nerves."

Other skinheads were also well aware of Tilbury's reputation for aggro, and their name was well-known down at The Last Resort skinhead emporium that was situated just off Petticoat Lane in East London. Saturday and Sunday were the busiest days, and all the skinheads would meet in various pubs around the shop. What pub usually depended on which ones would still serve skinheads, thanks to the trouble that usually accompanied them. And, more often that not, the trouble came in the shape of Tilbury's finest.

"In the end we ran out of pubs and all the skins were really getting fed up with us, but nobody had the bottle to take us on. One day in the shop, a group of skinheads told us to stop getting us all barred from everywhere for fighting, and my brother, Doghead, snapped back, 'That's what being a skinhead's all about you dickheads and if you don't like fighting then you shouldn't fucking be one.' That shut them up because my brother was very well-known and many people feared him in the shop."

With London on their doorstep, skinhead gigs were aplenty come the late Seventies and early Eighties. The Specials, Madness, and UB40 were playing as were the Oi! bands, and they also used to go and see the likes of Siouxsie & The Banshees and The Damned.

"You'd go down the youth club and the Ship," explained Panic, who organised coaches for some gigs, "and say where you were going on a Saturday night and to be on the seven o'clock train, and you'd have the mob from Tilbury get on that, get to Grays about ten past, and so it would go on, until there was maybe 100-150 skins on the train – all by word of mouth really."

Further notoriety came Tilbury's way in the shapely form of Oi! band Angela Rippon's Bum. In the early Eighties, the Tilbury lot were never far away if the likes of The Cockney Rejects or The 4 Skins were gigging, and it was only a matter of time before someone suggested forming a local band that everyone could follow and call their own. At the time, the Riverside Youth Centre was a popular haunt with local skins – Mick used to hold reggae discos there from time to time – and the warden said that they could have one of the rooms upstairs to practise in. It was Dave "Sticko" Strickson, the lead guitarist and only real talent, who came up with the name for no better reason than he liked the look of our Angela's arse.

Like everyone else and his dog, Mick White had auditioned for a place in the band without any initial luck, but after six months of watching from the sidelines, he was asked to manage the band. Like all good managers, a publicity campaign was number one on his list of how to get the band better known. Fly posters and graffiti did the job.

"Felt tip marker pens and spray cans were given out, and wherever they went, the Tilbury Skins would leave an Oi! Angela Rippon's Bum on a wall somewhere. I actually got caught and arrested myself for writing Angela Rippon's Bum on a wall. I was questioned as to why I'd write that and I explained it was the name of a band – they thought I was some sort of pervert or something."

Soon afterwards, the band went into the studio and recorded half a dozen songs, including the live favourites Skinheads Run Beserk and Bank Holidays, which found their way on to a demo cassette. It was sold to the Tilbury faithful and anyone else whose curiosity had been aroused by the band's name. It was also used to get gigs in and around London and soon the band were regularly gigging with the likes of The Business, Dagenham's The Ejected (whose Riot City single, Have You Got 10p, is their main claim to fame) and The Accused, a skinhead band from South Ockendon, about six miles from Tilbury. Garry Bushell reviewed one of their gigs at The Deuragon Arms, Hackney, for Sounds and described the Bum as "one of the very best skin – herbert bands doing the rounds."

Mick then came up with the classic idea of playing the tabloids at their own game. He phoned up The Sun and The Daily Mirror, pretending to be a middle-aged family man who admired Angela Rippon for her professionalism, and said he thought it was absolutely disgraceful that "a pop group" was allowed to name itself after the backside of a very respectable citizen. Mister Angry wanted Angela to be informed so that she could put a stop to these layabouts. Just as sure as day follows night, a reporter from The Sun was snooping about Tilbury within a few days, trying to track down the band. It wasn't difficult finding them either because two local skinhead girls, Big Jackie and Sandra, had more or less given their flat over to the Tilbury crew for parties, shagging and the like, and it had been renamed Oi! The House. Any kid could have pointed the reporter in the right direction.

The band was interviewed, and a week later the story had made The Sun and The Sunday People, and was also mentioned on national radio. On the back of all the publicity, and a few white lies to encourage clubs to book them, Angela Rippon's Bum was picking up gigs all over the place. A lot of gigs inevitably ended in punch ups thanks to their following of mainly skinheads who weren't slow at coming forward if there was any chance of aggro, and two ended as virtual riots. The first was at the Red Lion in Gravesend, Kent, which is just across the Thames from Tilbury. The Bum had already played there a couple of times with The Business, but this time they were booked to play with The Ovaltinies from South London.

"We had never heard of them as the pub had arranged it, but they turned up with a following of real right-wing British Movement skins and so it ended up in a real big fight and the place was smashed to bits. Good fun that one, but Angela Rippon's Bum was banned from playing there again though."

The second riot took place when the band was due to support The Last Resort (at what turned out to be the Resort's final gig) and ABH at Kings Lynn in Norfolk.

"We took a 50-seater coach full of followers with us plus some went in their own cars. Before the gig, we went into a local pub which was pretty packed with local herberts and it wasn't long before there was a really big row which spilled out onto the street. Nearby, we found a dairy with hundreds of crates full of empty bottles, and as the locals were coming out of the pub, we just continuously bombarded them. It went on for ages, the pub had no windows left, and there was just so much glass everywhere it was unbelievable. When the police finally arrived to spoil everything, they took the whole coachload in and held us over night because they had reason to believe one of our mob had stabbed a local who was now on the critical list. But next morning, when his condition became more stable and the police could not find out who stabbed him, they let us go."

The band was also a regular performer at Skunx at the Blue Coat Boy in Islington, a club opened in 1982 for punks and skins by Dave Long (later of Syndicate Records and other dodgy capers). It was there that they noticed quite a few skins and nearly all the punks were sniffing glue. Bass player, Kevin Earland, wrote a song called Glue Sniffing Kids which warned of the dangers of solvent abuse, and the band made it very clear that no glue sniffers were welcome at Angela Rippon's Bum gigs. Indeed, one of the dangers of doing glue was a good chance of getting a punch in the face from a Tilbury skin, but what they were saying was true. No true skinhead ever sniffed glue, and if you couldn't live without a glue bag then you're not a skin, you're a sad excuse for a punk.

"A lot of skinheads in 1981 started to sniff glue for some reason, and any skinheads that we ever saw sniffing glue, we used to bash. There were a lot of skinheads hanging around Soho and Leicester Square at the time, and they used to go sniffing glue in the alleys. Saturday nights, we used to go and wander around the West End, just bashing all the skinheads that used to sniff glue. While we were there, we would go up around Euston and King's Cross, where you get all the football supporters – Manchester, Liverpool, Leeds or whoever came down from up north to watch the London teams. We would walk up and down the Euston Road, fighting all the northern football supporters, and that was another little pastime."

The Tilbury took a lot of pride in themselves, not just as a firm, but as skinheads too. They always looked smart – tonic suits, ironed Ben Shermans, white Sta-press, polished boots – and were generally anti-drugs. In fact, quite a few of them were amateur boxers and so didn't even drink alcohol. Their buzz came from the natural high of being in a gang that always stood its ground and had the time of their lives.

Mickey French, the owner of The Last Resort, did ask the band to appear on one of his compilation albums, but they turned him down and ended up signing to Secret Records, appearing on the Back On The Streets EP with Fight For Your Lives, alongside four other bands. The band soldiered on until 1983, but following a fight between singer Tony Barker and a local skinhead, and with two of the band now fully fledged casuals, the decision was taken to call it a day. Angela Rippon's Bum might not have been the greatest band ever, but at least they put Tilbury on Oi! The Map and gave the local skins a band of their own to champion.

The reputation of the Tilbury lot brought them to the attention of the film industry, and as well as appearing in a couple of TV commercials, they ended up in Pink Floyd's The Wall, the film about the

S.A.S., Who Dares Wins, and also Madness' very own classic, Take It Or Leave It – as Chrissy Boy Foreman from the band remembers all too well.

"When we were filming what was supposed to be the gig at Acklam Hall, there was meant to be some trouble in the toilets, but instead of acting, you got the feeling they thought it was for real!"

"We'd like to be remembered as the most violent firm of skinheads there was," says Doghead, who has been stabbed a dozen times in fights and has the scars to prove it too. "Pakis, blacks, Nazis, whoever got in our way, we'd bash. In them days, we used to go out and have a fight or whatever, but now a few of us have got educated and now we work as nightclub bouncers and get paid for it. We still love violence."

Pakis and Asians in general were generally hated by the Tilbury mob. As far as they are concerned, they shouldn't be in the country. It's as simple as that.

"It was the in thing to do," recalls Bomber. "Have your hair cropped, get a pair of boots, and go and bash pakis."

While a lot of other skinheads were sporting NF or BM badges, the Tilbury came up with their own variation on the racist theme – The Anti-Paki League. They regularly went paki-bashing in the East End of London and were mainly responsible for the 1977 Brick Lane riots that made the headlines as skinheads ran amok, attacking Asians.

"I love Fifties rock 'n' roll," explains Mick White, "but the reason I didn't become a teddy boy was because everyone knew skinheads didn't like pakis and I thought that's the one for me."

Although the Tilbury Trojan Skins have never made any bones about their hatred for Asians, that doesn't make them Nazis – the label no doubt any trendy lefty reading this is mentally pinning on the Tilbury skinheads this very moment.

"If you're a skinhead and you say you don't like someone, whether it's pakis or not, you're classed as a Nazi," reckons Panic. "You can't even wear your flag with pride now because as soon as you put a Union Jack on or a St. George's cross, you have people saying you're a Nazi. But in other countries, like America, they have their flag outside their house. They're proud of their country. Do it in this country – you're labelled a Nazi."

Mick naturally agrees. "There's no way we're Nazis. My father fought Nazis in the war. All our Dads did. The APL was different. Just because I hate pakis, doesn't make me a Nazi."

The fact was, the Tilbury skins weren't the least bit interested in politics. Hating pakis was no different to hating glue sniffers or hating students. What's more, they hated Nazis too, and took equal pleasure in thumping them, as the trouble at the gig with The Olvaltinies described earlier testifies.

"Another time, at the Electric Ballroom in Camden Town, we all went to see Bad Manners and all the British Movement were there. Although we hated pakis and sikhs and that, we also didn't like Nazis as our parents fought them in the war. We couldn't understand why skins should be connected to them as our idea of skinhead is to be British and proud of it, and all other cunts are the enemy, including Germans. Anyway, we hated the British Movement and had had trouble with them before at the famous Bridge House in Canning Town, and again the Tilbury Skins showed their might at the Ballroom and showed them who the real bosses were."

Most of the Tilbury Trojan Skins are in their thirties now and have settled down with wives, kids, what have you. But the passion for the cult is still there. Some are still skinheads and others are not, but as any half decent ex-skin will tell you, you might grow your hair, but it doesn't change your heart.

"What made us special was we stuck together," Mick explained. "We were a hundred strong and we all stuck together. Even today, you could make a few phone calls and if you are in trouble – boomp – there's 30 or 40 of us there."

Some of the Tilbury, like Mick, Brian Archer, Steve Worldly, and a few others have been skinheads since the late Sixties and early Seventies. Others have stayed true to the cult since joining in the late Seventies and early Eighties. Skinheads come and go in most areas, but for one reason or another, there have always been skinheads in Tilbury. It must be something in the water, but whatever it is, it should be available on tap in every pub in the country if it is going to keep the cult alive and kicking.

About every two months, a reggae dance is held in a working men's club in Tilbury and it's a chance for the old crew to meet up for a drink and a dance. It's run by Steve Wordly who plays nothing but reggae and ska all night. At a recent dance, someone asked him to play a chart hit and he put an announcement out saying, "Just to let you know this is a reggae night and that's all we're going to play, mostly old ska for all the skinheads that are here. And if you don't like it, don't bother coming in."

The Tilbury crew was a lot more typical of skinheads in the late Seventies and early Eighties than most people would care to remember, and that's particularly true of skinheads in and around London. They would have been well at home in the late Sixties too when paki-bashing first hit the headlines, but the important distinction is that they have nothing in common with the further shift towards extremism that started in the early Eighties and came to fruition later that decade with organisations like the neo-Nazi Blood And Honour.

Nearly all skinheads are proud of their country, and some (but certainly not all) are also racist. Far fewer though believe that Adolf Hitler was right and that's particularly true in Britain. That point is borne out by the fact that skinhead numbers have fallen with every shift towards the extreme right. Blood And Honour has far less support than the Young National Front used to carry, and the numbers the YNF and British Movement could muster were far fewer than the number of skinheads who turned up on a Saturday afternoon to watch a Second Division football match in 1970, when politics and skinheads led separate lives.

Paki-bashing during the late Sixties was very much of its time, when British society was still very insular in its views, still very much an island, still very proud of its once mighty Empire and successes in two World Wars and one World Cup (well, south of the border anyway). Thousands had given their lives to defeat Nazi Germany, but it was a war fought to defend British interests and sovereignty and not to defeat national socialism (just as the Gulf War was about oil, not Iraqi tyranny).

Racism was alive and well before, during, and after Adolf Hitler, and that was as true in Great Britain as it was anywhere else in the world. There was a general feeling that politician Enoch Powell had got it right with his Rivers Of Blood speech of 1968 which predicted racial violence as competition for jobs and houses intensified, and this was particularly true in the working class areas where Asian immigrants first settled and where skinheads first appeared.

Paki-bashing was as much a cultural issue as it was a race one, if not more so. The first generation of Asian immigrants was different – they didn't try to integrate, they kept themselves to themselves, some couldn't even speak the language, and of course, they were easy targets because they didn't fight back. It was a culture clash that led to them being singled out as easy targets, and it wasn't just skinheads or even born and bred British white working class kids doing the bashing. Black kids were at it too as were the Greeks and other minorities who had done more to adapt to the British way of life. Even more to the point, some of the blacks involved in paki-bashing were fully fledged skinheads themselves.

"The first skinheads I remember were called peanuts," recalls Arthur Kay, famous in skinhead circles as the founder of cult ska band Arthur Kay & The Originals and as the bass player with the Oi!some The Last Resort. "There were hundreds of them in Streatham and the area. Every youth club was playing ska and reggae and every skinhead firm had a few caribs, a few Jamaican guys. You all used to go to the same clubs and there was never a problem."

"It wasn't just white kids bashing Asians," adds Chris Prete, "it was everybody bashing everybody to be top dog in the street, and unfortunately it was the Asians who came out worse. The media picked up on that and gave it a lot of publicity."

Lots of skinheads lived in areas where there were no Asians anyway, so tabloid headlines were as close to beating up immigrants as those skins ever got.

"We never went paki-bashing because there weren't any up here," recalls Graham from Bridlington. "Too cold for them! We used to go Wessy bashing – bashing day-trippers and holidaymakers from West Riding."

And then of course, there were plenty of skinheads who didn't agree with paki-bashing anyway.

"I had some skinhead friends come up to visit where I'd just moved to," recalls Gaz Mayall, "and one of them, a guy called John Marsh, went up to a kid by a sandpit in the park, a little Asian boy. He walked up to him, attracted his attention, the kid turned around, and John just head butted him, knocking him out there and then on the spot. And I felt outraged and I cut myself off from John Marsh there and then. I don't think I've ever seen him since."

Media coverage of paki-bashing no doubt increased the number of attacks, but it was never politically orchestrated or organised. The booklet that accompanied Channel 4's Walk On The Wild Side series states that in February 1967, "Three of Britain's neo-fascist groups merge to form the National Front. The national media quickly identify the party as the home of the newly-evolved skinhead movement."

That is absolute bollocks. For a good few years after its birth, the National Front was so far removed from mainstream life, it might as well have been on the moon. Nobody had ever heard of them, let alone supported them, during the days of the original skinhead. Voicing support for Mr. Powell was about as political as they got.

"People harp on about the old days and in the Sixties and stuff like that with the reggae music," says Paul Burnley. "Even back then there were racist skinheads, but not so much affiliated to political parties. In the late Seventies and Eighties, and as of now, the connection is definitely there."

It wasn't until the National Front began to achieve any level of success that the skinhead cult was dragged into politics for the first time. In the 1977 local elections, the National Front received over 250,000 votes, and over a third of that total was counted in London polling stations. Most skinheads weren't even old enough to vote and so represented a very small proportion of those voters. More old grannies probably voted NF than skinheads, but from that moment on the cult was to be associated with racism in the tiny minds of those who are very good at pointing the finger in our direction while the far more complex issues of racism go largely unchallenged.

Although you had the Anti-Nazi League branding all NF members and supporters as fascists and Nazis, in reality very few were. It was a vote for Great Britain, the Union Jack, and a protest vote against the Conservative and Labour parties who had done little in real terms for the British working classes who were now facing longer dole queues, shit housing, and a country going to the dogs.

Teenagers wouldn't be teenagers if they weren't hitting out at authority, and a lot of National Front support at the time came from kids looking to play the hard man, wanting to hit out at society. Life's a bastard, and kids will always cover up their own insecurities by hitting out at soft targets, whether that's a fat boy, the school smellies, the new girl, or the kid in the corner with a turban on his head. Chants of "National Front!" echoed around playgrounds because it gave you a sense of belonging, a sense of power, a sense of defiance, and not because you had read the NF's manifesto and agreed with every word.

Part of the National Front's attraction was the very fact that teachers, parents, and other authority figures told you not to do it. Just like they told you not to smoke, drink bottles of cider over the park, nick sweets from the corner shop, go looking for trouble at the football. For their part, the Front did the exact opposite, hailing skinheads and football hooligans as the cream of British youth, ready to take on Johnny Foreigner in the football stadiums of Europe and in the back streets of Britain. It's human nature to gravitate towards those who accept you and to back away from those who condemn you.

"Politicians will go for the skinhead cult because of the passion involved," reckons Symond, "so it's easy for an extreme party to grab hold of passionate kids – whether it's the Nazis, the lefties, the Ban The Bomb lot. People like skinheads were very angry, and so for the extremists, they were easy targets, easy to pick up, and they'd say, 'Believe what we say, and you'll be with us and fight for us' – and you would have done."

It is also true that white working class kids are becoming increasingly alienated in today's society. There are housing estates in Britain today where you've more chance of winning the national lottery than you do of finding a job. Increased support for the extreme right is definitely connected with this sense of alienation, but rather than deal with the root causes – ignorance, unemployment, poor housing, poverty, and discrimination – the powers that be seek to alienate them further. White kids are just as hard done by, just as disadvantaged as black kids. Do-gooders can whine all they want to, but the fact is that the vast majority of people living below the poverty line in Britain today are white. There is no positive discrimination for poor whites though.

"In Newcastle, there's a place called the Newcastle Young Black Persons Association," says Graham, a non-racist skin from the city, "but there is no Newcastle Young White Persons Association. Now, if everybody's going to be equal, there should be a Newcastle Young White Persons Association."

If you're white, on the dole, living in a damp flat, and you get told someone else has got the job you wanted for no other reason than he is black, it can only be seen as racism in reverse.

"Young white kids have got nothing," says Paul Burnley. "Nobody is standing up for them. Nobody is saying they should have this and they should have that, but they are for blacks, Asians, queers, and God knows what else."

Bulldog, the paper of the Young National Front, must have sold thousands of copies every issue, mainly at football matches and at gigs, and especially in London and other big cities. Edited by Joe Pearce, who was jailed twice for inciting racial hatred through its pages, and then by the mysterious Captain Truth, each issue rarely stretched beyond six pages, but as a vehicle for the YNF, it was perfect. Its political content was blunt, basic and crude, but at the same time incredibly effective. By focusing on stories about black terror gangs, positive discrimination towards immigrants for jobs and houses, and Asians coming here and living on the dole, they portrayed a version of events that, while not truly representative or indeed the complete picture, certainly rang a few bells with a lot of white working class kids. After all, they were being treated like shit by the powers that be, and it was only the Young National Front and the British Movement who seemed to be talking to them and for them.

"I had some mates in Birmingham," says Brian Kelson of the era, "and they dressed smart, but were National Front. I used to explain to them why I wasn't National Front, because of the Nazis and that, but they said they wanted to make a point. It's all right for you, they'd say, living out in suburbia in a white community, but we live in the middle of Birmingham in a mixed race society. We didn't invite them here, the government invited them here, not us, and we don't want them here. They're taking our jobs and everything, and this is the only way we can make our voices heard. Perhaps they had a point. Perhaps if I'd lived there and it'd affected me, I might be more like them. I know if I lose my job, I become more racist. Not in the sense of thinking our race is better than them and they deserve to be obliterated or anything, but you get to thinking three million foreigners in the country and three million unemployed, it makes sense. You do get a bit bitter when you're unemployed. Unemployment brings out the worst in everybody, and a lot of skinheads are from inner city areas and are unemployed. So I can see their point of view, but I still wish they'd get their own cult to voice it rather than taking our cult and using it!"

It wasn't just skinheads either who gave their support to the YNF – mods, casuals, herberts, punks and others did too, as a letter in a 1982 issue from the Spurs NF clearly showed, as do any photos of NF marches from the era. Again, it's a media myth that every Front march was dominated by skinheads.

Usually, a couple of pages of every issue of Bulldog were devoted to music. Naturally enough, skinhead music took top billing, and Oi! was regularly featured, helping to lay the foundations for the often-repeated media myth that Oi! is by definition racist rock. The truth was, Bulldog would feature any band that had a skinhead following and that even included bands like Bad Manners who had a black and two Jews in their line up. At the time, 2 Tone and related bands like Madness and Manners were playing a hybrid of black music, and doing more to promote racial harmony just by playing than the ANL has ever achieved – just as today, the likes of Ferdinand, Cole, Fortune-West, Collymore, Wright, blah, blah, blah, make it difficult for the extreme right to make much headway on the football terraces (despite what the media tells you about all football hooligans being Nazis).

That said, part of the ska bands' following came from Young National Front supporters, and this was particularly true of gigs in and around London – less so the further north you moved.

"I remember coming out of a Bad Manners gig at the Rainbow in North London and about 500 skinheads came out and walked under this archway, sieg heiling and stuff, and a few blacks got beaten up. There was always a high presence of right-wing, and never any suggestion of left-wing, even though the 2 Tone thing could probably be traced back to the black and white thing."

"It was very difficult to do anything to promote racial harmony," Madness' Chrissy Boy remembers. "We used to get a lot of stick for not really coming out with some sort of political agenda, but we used to try and talk to some of these people (who followed the NF) and find out why they thought like that."

What's more, other bands with not even the remotest connection with the National Front would regularly appear in its pages because of some obscure connection. Spandau Ballet were hailed as a great new band for white youth for no other reason that Spandau prison in Germany housed the leading Nazi, Rudolf Hess, at the time. Others like The Clash (because of White Riot), and The Dentists (Master Race) regularly appeared in Rock Against Communism charts – as did Bing Crosby for, you guessed it, White Christmas!

In fact, it wasn't until May '83 – long after the heyday of both 2 Tone and Oi! – that Bulldog could say, "at last a band have come along with the courage of their convictions… Skrewdriver." They had, in fact, missed the first ever Rock Against Communism gig because of "record company pressure" (they were signed to Manchester indie label, TJM, at the time), but by now they were headlining gigs with like-minded bands like The Ovaltinies and Peter & The Wolves.

Seeing the potential of music as both a crowd puller and a fund raiser at a time when National Front support generally had totally collapsed, the NF quickly launched the White Noise label with a Skrewdriver EP called White Power. A fanzine, Rocking The Reds, was also started, but it was a very poor alternative to the mainstream media that had virtually blacked all news about NF bands (that said, NME did review White Power, although hardly favourably) and was quickly absorbed into the pages of Bulldog. Bulldog survived until 1985, when internal power struggles saw it disappear and then be replaced by the "revolutionary voice of British youth", New Dawn. Somehow, it lacked the edge that Bulldog had possessed – the regular coverage of football violence had gone for a start – and it never really took off in the same way.

By then, the YNF was dead on its feet anyway and White Noise Records had been reduced to joint ventures with the German Rock-O-Rama Records. What's more, falling support in Britain saw the WNC reach out to whites overseas for additional support. 10 bands and six hundred people did turn up for a Rock Against Communism festival in Suffolk later that year, but the jailing of Skrewdriver's Ian Stuart and the later discovery that the White Noise Club had been ripping off both bands and fans finally called time on the Young National Front.

By the summer of '87, leading bands on the white power scene had broken away to form Blood And Honour, an organisation that produced a magazine of the same name. Issue one was for all nationalist music fans, but as early as issue two Blood And Honour was describing itself as "the National Socialist music paper". In September, a gig in London saw Skrewdriver, Brutal Attack, No Remorse, and Sudden Impact formally launch the new organisation which, at least until the death of Ian Stuart in a car crash in 1993, dominated the white power music world.

"The death of Ian Stuart was a big blow and it'll still be a few years before the patriotic music scene recovers", reckons Paul Burnley. "It's back to square one, building again. There's a lot of good music about and the scene's concentrating on a more world-wide scale. We're looking outside of the UK to see an upsurge of right-wing music and there will be a major breakthrough in coming years."

That remains to be seen, but as Paul says, that breakthrough isn't likely to come in the UK. And it's certainly not likely to come in towns like Tilbury. The Tilbury Skins don't see anything patriotic about Nazi rock music. They might hate pakis and they might be racists, but like the vast majority of Britons, they will never dance to the tune of Adolf Hitler.

Ghost Town

Detroit, Michigan, is a city fighting for its very survival. It is known throughout the world as Motor City, home of the automobile industry, but today it is a shadow of its former self, almost a ghost town symbolised by a giant railway station that lies abandoned and derelict in what was once the centre of the city.

Inner city decline in the Detroit of the Fifties and Sixties was hastened by the so-called "white flight" after the riots of 1967 which claimed 54 lives. Those who could afford to move to the more affluent areas around Detroit did so, resulting in businesses closing, further decline, and more people leaving. The end result was a city that had lost half of its population and most of its wealth. Today, it's a city of have-nots, three quarters of whom are black and captives of a form of racial segregation based on economics. In fact, many white people from the suburbs boast that they haven't been to Detroit for years except to see the Red Wings or the Tigers play.

Like all industrial cities, Detroit has always been a tough, uncompromising place to be. It's no surprise that its streets have given birth to world class boxers like Sugar Ray Robinson, Thomas "The Hit Man" Hearns, and the legendary Brown Bomber, Joe Louis – heavyweight champion of the world for an incredible 13 years.

Another professional boxer and former Ford assembly line worker who went on to find both fame and fortune was Berry Gordy, whose Tamla Motown empire put Detroit on the musical map under the name of Hitsville, USA. Almost as if to underline the decline of this once great city, even Motown has vacated its premises and moved to the sunnier climes of Los Angeles. All that's left are the memories and a museum. Not only has the heart of the city packed its bags and headed for the suburbs, but the soul has now gone too.

The sound of Motown was incredibly popular with the original skinheads, just as it had been with the mods of a few years before, and remains so today in traditional skinhead circles. The likes of The

Miracles, The Four Tops, The Marvelletes, and The Supremes have a home in many a skinhead's record collection, and of course many skinhead reggae classics are in fact covers of soul songs, including Bob & Marcia's Young, Gifted And Black (Harry J) which had originally been recorded by Nina Simone and then Aretha Franklin. Indeed, it's no coincidence that Motown enjoyed some of its best chart success in the UK during the skinhead's golden era of 1968 to 1972.

In Detroit, you won't find too many people who would associate skinheads with their beloved Tamla Motown though. In fact, if the local media hysteria that surrounded a triple murder is to be believed, Detroit's music beats a totally different drum as far as skinheads are concerned today. Move over Motown gems like Martha And The Vandella's Dancing In The Street (which also appeared on Stateside) and Marvin Gaye's I Heard It Through The Grapevine. And make way for new skinhead anthems like White, Straight & Proud by New Minority and Nordic Thunder's Born To Hate.

The murder case in question concerned two skinhead brothers from Allentown, Pennsylvania, Bryan and David Freeman, who beat and stabbed their parents and younger brother to death in February, 1995. They were eventually caught in Midland, a town about one hundred miles to the north of Detroit, which accounted for some of the local interest. The media, naturally enough, looked for the sensationalist angle and from the press and TV coverage, you would have thought that the brothers' main crime was their association with the skinhead cult – the fact that they murdered three people came a poor second.

Media portrayals of the two brothers made them look more like extras from The Hills Have Eyes than skinheads. Both had the word Berserkr tattooed on their foreheads which did little to enhance this image. Berserkr is the name of a white power metal band from Oklahoma which had risen from the ashes of the Mid-Town Bootboys, a skinhead band from the late Eighties whose progress had been abruptly halted when band members ended up on the wrong side of prison bars. It just so happened that Berserkr's debut album, The Voice Of Our Ancestors, had just been released by Detroit-based Resistance Records, a label that from a standing start in early 1994 has quickly made its way to the forefront of the white power music scene.

Resistance Records was started by 25-year-old Canadian George Birdi, who goes under the name of George E. Hawthorne, and who is the singer with hard rock band, Rahowa, an abbreviation of the slogan Racial Holy War. The story goes that a farm was mortgaged to finance the label's launch, but there can be little doubt that financial support must also have been forthcoming from other quarters to get the ball rolling so quickly and so professionally.

In fact, the registered address for Resistance Records is no more than a small and empty office suite in Detroit itself. None of that takes away from the fact that for the first time, and particularly in the USA, white power music has a platform it can be justly proud of.

Resistance quickly signed leading American white power bands like Detroit's own Max Resist & The Hooligans, Wisconsin's Centurion, and Maryland's Bound For Glory. Since then, other bands have been added to the label's roster, including Britain's very own No Remorse. The music varies in style from Nordic Thunder's hardcore-Oi! sound to Aggravated Assault's "Racial Shock Rock" to New Minority who apparently sound like "Skid Row or Motley Crue" and aren't embarrassed to admit it.

Rahowa's latest album, Cult Of The Holy War, is described as "fascist neo-classical gothic metal" – try saying that after a few pints – but one thing they all have in common is the superb packaging that rivals that of any mainstream label.

In the UK, from the days of the Young National Front's Bulldog magazine right through to Blood & Honour, white power music has been promoted in a halfway house format, somewhere between amateurism and professionalism. The same has been true of record and CD releases, although at least in this department standards have been improving over the years. Rock-O-Rama Records, based in Brühl, Germany, was until recently the biggest name in white power music (although they also sold other types of street music including punk, ska and reggae through their catalogue – a point rarely made in any circles), but the police raids during 1993 that formed part of the crackdown on German neo-Nazi activity, have had a definite effect on its output. That, together with the death of Skrewdriver's Ian Stuart, left a massive vacuum – and one that is quickly being filled by Resistance Records.

The label also publishes the glossy magazine, Resistance – again a publication that wouldn't look out of place on any newsagent's shelves. A big problem for street music in general is that it tends to be confined to the realms of fanzine land. That's all well and good for the faithful die-hards who can see beyond the often poorly-photocopied pages, but the danger is that bands with the potential to reach a far wider audience don't do so. Resistance magazine's full-colour cover, professional design, and well-written articles go a long way to making you think that maybe the bands are as good as its glossy pages would have you believe.

Just as important, for anyone preaching white power, is the fact that the quality of the product might help to persuade people that the articles on race and related issues just might hold something too. It's no great secret of history that aspiring political movements have always looked to youth for support, and what better way to reach out to them than through music. Resistance Magazine obviously has a part to play in winning the hearts and minds of its readers, casual or committed, to the white power cause, again a role made all the more important following the demise of Tom Metzger's White Aryan Resistance and Ben Klassen's Church Of The Creator, the latter a white supremacist organisation which declares that "Our race is our religion" and advocates the Racial Holy War that gave its name to George Hawthorne's band.

Ben Klassen's death has obviously affected the running of his church, and Metzger's WAR was supposedly brought to its knees in 1990 when a court found Metzger and his son guilty of inciting the violence that led to the killing of an Ethiopian man in Portland, Oregon, by WAR skinheads.

The victim's family was awarded a staggering $12.5 million in damages, and the Metzgers lost their family home and personal property as a result. WAR certainly hasn't been put out of business as was widely-predicted would happen, but it is equally true that it has lost much of its power, for the time being anyway.

That really leaves Resistance to fly the flag among the young, and it is doing so with considerable evangelism. It claims a circulation of 13,000 copies an issue for its magazine and uses its pages to promote its own and like-minded bands as well as the white power message. Next to interviews with No Remorse and Bound For Glory you'll find features like an "Introduction To The Ku Klux Klan", "Interview With A Black Separatist", and "Charles Manson: Has He Been Misunderstood?". It makes for entertaining reading in the main, although obviously only one perspective is put forward, and truth, as always, is in the eye of the beholder.

One article claimed to dismiss the idea that the skinhead cult was born in the late Sixties by advocating that it had its roots in Oswald Mosley's brown shirts of the 1930s! The same article also conveniently makes no reference to skinhead reggae, but hails Motörhead – of all bands – as a great skinhead band of the Seventies! This sort of nonsense may be believed in certain circles in the USA, but here in Old Blighty where people know the score, it just won't wash. For the record, Motörhead is a heavy metal band whose only distant connection with the skinhead cult is that their drummer, Phil Taylor, used to be one.

The evangelism of Resistance's message also brings to mind the preachers that pollute American TV, bringing you the word of God in the hope that you'll send them some money. Resistance doesn't ask for donations as such – but they are keen to let you know that by buying their CDs, magazines, and t-shirts, you will be advancing the cause of the white race. All that said, if everyone in street circles did as much as Resistance to promote their own brand of music, we might not have to put up with the likes of Elton John and Cliff Richard any longer.

The media hasn't been slow to afford Resistance Records massive publicity either. MTV's Hate Rock special must have done wonders for Resistance bands like Aryan (who were filmed at their first ever gig), and CNN also did a 12-minute feature on Resistance Records which included footage of Rahowa in the studio. In addition to TV coverage, features in magazines and newspapers have all added to a wave of publicity, something that fuels the fires that burn deep inside everyone with a gospel to spread.

Being linked with the Freeman brothers might not be everyone's idea of top dollar publicity, but when your music is being played on prime time TV, any publicity has to be good. You also don't have to have a degree in psychology to know that the forbidden fruit is the most tempting of all.

"When I was younger, I always had problems with blacks at school, so I had animosity towards blacks and minorities, so the politics really attracted me," says Chris of Baltimore. "And when I read about white power skins, it was something I wanted to do. It seemed like it was really good, like a brotherhood."

The media's focus on the underground, rebellious, volatile, and extremist nature of white power music acts like a magnet for disaffected youngsters who rarely share authority figure concerns and desires. The fact that you can't buy the records and CDs in most local record shops simply adds to the attraction.

A classic case of this was the hype that surrounded the 1992 Aussie film, Romper Stomper. Made with a budget of less than a million pounds (small change in movie terms), it was never really destined for big things – until the media, aided and abetted by anti-fascist groups, gave it the sort of coverage that money just can't buy, resulting in lots of curious people wanting to see this film for themselves.

It wasn't a film about skinheads. It was a film about an outsider's impression of neo-Nazi skinheads. Most commentators and punters probably missed the distinction, but there obviously is one and a big one at that. Particularly for skinheads. A great many skins don't see anything resembling themselves in the film, and as sure as night follows day, that will include a lot of neo-Nazi skinheads.

Romper Stomper was an action-packed journey into the world of a neo-Nazi skinhead gang based in Melbourne. As these things go, it was far better than the appallingly pathetic Greydon Clark's Skinheads, but never got close to the likes of A Clockwork Orange in the cult classic stakes (although writer and director Geoffrey Wright had obviously helped himself to more than one or two ideas from Kubrik's benchmark masterpiece). The chances are, Romper Stomper would have received very limited cinema exposure before being condemned to a life on the dusty shelves of video rental shop shelves. But rather than let that happen, the likes of the Anti-Nazi League organised an hysterical campaign against the film, saying that it promoted Nazism and would lead to copy-cat violence, blah, blah, blah.

The media then turned its spotlight on this shock horror film, and before you knew it, Romper Stomper was on release throughout the country, followed by a long spell in the video charts. Efforts to ban it had ultimately led to the film's success. The hypocrisy of the placard-wielding moral guardians standing outside cinemas in a bid to stop people seeing Romper Stomper was almost deafening. The chosen few among the protesters who had seen it arrogantly sought to deny the right of others to make up their own minds about the film. Most of them hadn't even seen the film, and so didn't have a clue as to what they were protesting about. A case of the blind attempting to lead the blind.

On Romper Stomper's opening night in Copenhagen, Denmark, 23 skinheads were attacked as they left the cinema by around 100 demonstrators armed with sticks, iron bars, bottles, and CS gas. The skins were chased into a nearby hotel where they armed themselves with chairs, beer glasses, and fire extinguishers. A street fight raged before the police arrived and two demonstrators ended up in hospital – one after being thrown through a shop window, the other after his own CS Gas was sprayed in his face. If the skinheads had seen the film and then gone on the rampage, you would have heard about it in Timbuktu. As it was, only one Danish national newspaper featured the incident.

The media's linking of Resistance Records to the Freeman brothers via dodgy Indian ink tattoos seems to be yet another example of tabloid journalism at its very worst. Like them or loathe them, Resistance Records had as much to do with the murder case as the makers of the brothers' underwear did. Or for that matter, as much to do with the murders as the skinhead cult in general. As Ryan, a skinhead who lived near the brothers put it, "What does murdering your family have to do with being a skin? They did it because they were twisted losers, not because they're skins."

Skinheads are used to tabloid bullshit like this the world over. In March, 1994, Keith Wilkinson walked into a school in Middlesbrough and stabbed three young girls, killing one of them. Three days before Wilkinson attacked those kids, he decided to shave his head. The tabloid newspapers in Britain had a field day because not only was this man a knife-wielding maniac, he was now a skinhead too! The implication being, of course, that the skinhead haircut had something to do with his actions.

Even their own articles made it clear to anyone with half a brain that Wilkinson was not a skinhead, describing him as a loner, who had never worked and never had a girlfriend, and as someone who spent his time in his bedroom playing computer games and listening to heavy metal. The Daily Star said all of this, and even ran a quarter page feature on his favourite band, Iron Maiden (a band with even fewer skinhead links than Motörhead). And yet this same newspaper refers to "skinhead Wilkinson" and has a headline that screamed, He Looked So Evil With Skinhead Haircut. In fact, a neighbour told The Daily Mail that "he looked the hippy type and certainly played heavy metal."

The Sun too was at it with the heading, SKINHEAD LONER WHO LIVED FOR HEAVY METAL HORROR SONGS AND COMPUTERS, only they had his favourite band down as Sepultura, that well-known Brazilian death metal band. You could fill an entire book on how the British media has misrepresented the skinhead cult. And then you could go on to fill hundreds of others on how it had misrepresented other groups and individuals over the years.

But back to the States for the time being. The Anti-Defamation League, which monitors skinhead activity, reckons there to be around 3,500 racist skinheads in the USA. The media frenzy over their activities, particularly in the late Eighties when they were even appearing on the likes of The Oprah Winfrey Show and Geraldo, is totally out of all proportion to their numbers and actions. To put things in perspective, there are over 100,000 gang members in the Los Angeles area alone. Skinhead-related violence in the land of the free is but a drop in the ocean of blood spilled every year in gang-banging, but it's the skinheads who will get the column inches in the newspapers the next day. The kid in a body bag as a result of black on black violence will be remembered by graffiti on the walls of his 'hood and on page 63 of the local newspaper, if he is lucky.

I mean, for fuck's sake! An estimated 135,000 juveniles carry guns to school every day in the USA. That should frighten the hell out of right-on America, but they're too busy making placards for the next Nazis Out rally. Again, according to the Anti-Defamation League, 40 murders have been attributed to "racist skinheads" since the late Eighties. 40 murders is 40 murders too many, but why do the people who are so outraged by these deaths spend so little energy fighting gang violence which can clock up 40 deaths over a good weekend?

It's almost as if black kids shooting each other doesn't really matter. And it's almost as if the biggest crime in the politically correct world of today is to hold racist beliefs. You can be a drug dealer, a rapist or a child molester, but as long as you aren't a Nazi that's okay. And you can drive aid convoys to Bosnia (as one BNP supporting skin did, risking his own life to bring food and comfort to a largely forgotten people) and you will still be classed as scum of the Earth by the right-on brigade if you hold racist beliefs.

There can be no doubt that the acres of publicity donated by the media and anti-fascist groups to white power organisations like Resistance represents one of their biggest recruitment tools. So the very people who claim to be taking a stand against racism also supply the oxygen of publicity that guarantees its very survival and growth.

There is also little doubt that the continuous media focus on skinheads – arguably the most visible and frightening face of white power beyond the hoods and gowns of the Ku Klux Klan – and their links with the extreme right has created the impression that all skinheads support racist or Nazi or white power organisations. And of course, journalists look to past articles and features for research material and continue to make the link to the point where the words "skinhead" and "Nazi" mean virtually the same thing in media circles.

As Cock Sparrer sing (with tongue firmly planted in side of mouths), The Sun says, The Sun says, so it must be true.

Virtually everyone reading this has political views of one sort or another. We are certainly all affected by the world of politics, so it makes sense to have an idea of what the powers that be are doing in your name. Skinheads, just like everyone else, have the right to believe, say and do whatever they want, just as long as they don't infringe on the rights of others to live in peace and do likewise. And, if that includes buying white power records, then good luck to them.

Me, I'm the world's worst. I've got an opinion on everything. Sit me in front of the TV news and within twenty seconds I'm moaning about this and correcting that. Deciding everything from doctors' pay to who'll be the next heavyweight champion of the world in seconds. The ultimate armchair dictator. Alf Garnett's running mate. Why they pay politicians thousands of pounds a year, I'll never know, because I could screw things up just as badly for the price of a few beers. Every election, be it local or national, and I toddle off to the polling booth to cast my vote. Every election, come rain or shine, I'll be there. Some issues I believe strongly in, some I couldn't care less about. My beliefs and opinions have been shaped by my family, my friends, my upbringing, what I see, hear, and read, and my experiences of life. They will continue to be so until my last breath on this fair planet.

But one thing that has never influenced my thinking – and this will come as a surprise to most journalists – is the length of my hair. Shaving my head does not change who I am. When the razor runs over your scalp, you get a haircut, not a brain transplant. Nobody is born a skinhead (despite what the odd tattoo might tell you) and there is nobody from quality control standing on the door telling people who can and who can't become a skinhead. Different aspects of the cult attract different people, and just as with any other group within society, you get a cross-section of views and opinions. Such is the spice of life.

There's no doubting that there are racist skinheads, fascist skinheads, white power skinheads, what have you. But there is equally no doubting that there are anti-racist skinheads, anti-fascist skinheads, and skinheads who judge you by the colour of your football scarf and not by the colour of your skin. And then there are all the skinheads in between, with their various opinions and beliefs, and there are plenty more who basically couldn't care less about politics, full stop. To some, a two pence rise in the price of a pint of beer is more important than a change of government, and who's to say they're wrong?

You pays your money in this life, and you takes your choice. And that's true of skinheads, football hooligans, bus drivers, accountants, vicars, vegetarians or any other group within society you want to single out. The powers that be though, the powers that would like to be, and the mugs who hang on their every word, have every skinhead down as a "Nazi". If you actually ask them what a Nazi is, most of them don't have a clue, and it must be one of the most overused and misused labels of today. If you can't even define the problem, don't pretend you've got the perfect solution.

If you're white, working class, and wearing an England football top, chances are some fool somewhere has you down as a Nazi. Sounds ridiculous, but such is the misplaced hysteria of today's politically correct tub thumpers.

The riot in Dublin which caused the Ireland versus England friendly to be abandoned was a case in point. Even those who claimed football hooliganism was a thing of the past – either because they didn't have a clue what they were talking about or because they didn't want to upset the gravy train that Euro '96 would bring to England the following year – must have realised that there was the potential for trouble at such a game.

But, as is so often the case, the authorities were caught with their pants down. Not to worry though, let's just blame "skinheads" and "extremists" and pretend we've got everything under control for the European Championships.

Very few skinheads were even at the game. There were a lot of people there with shaved heads because it is one of the most popular haircuts of today, but they aren't skinheads and neither do they see themselves as such. Dressed head to toe in Armani, Ralph Lauren, Duffer, and Adidas, it's hardly surprising.

The extremists who supposedly organised the trouble were Combat 18, the London-based Nazi organisation that the media just can't stop talking about. The reality of football violence in the UK though is that the vast majority of hooligans have no political affiliations whatsoever. And although some, no doubt, do support the extreme right, there are also others who are on the other side of the street with the likes of Anti-Fascist Action and Red Action.

Of course, England fans are going to sing "No surrender to the IRA" at a match against Ireland, just like Scotland fans chanted "What's it like to lose a war?" the last time Argentina came to Hampden Park. The Dublin songs were obviously coloured by events in Northern Ireland and mainland Britain, but to suggest they were all part and parcel of the extremists' arsenal is complete and utter nonsense.

The Herald newspaper recently ran a photo that was taken at the Dublin game that claimed to portray "English fans with neo-Nazi symbols on their flags" giving sieg heil salutes. There are four flags in the photo: one Union Jack from Wallsend and three St. George crosses. The only visible symbol is the crossed hammers of West Ham. Some of the crowd, which includes a young kid and a few old men, have hands in the air, but all but one have clenched fists. Fans the world over pump the air with their fists as they sing, and it's plain to see that this is exactly what was going on in this photograph.

Years ago, during a radio commentary of a Brighton game, the commentators were saying how sickened they were to hear sieg heil chants from the terraces. In fact, the fans were chanting "Seagulls!" – Brighton's nickname. A not so funny anecdote when you read in The Guardian that a similar mistake was made by the police who mounted an eight month investigation into a Combat 18 style firm at the Goldstone Ground chanting Nazi slogans at every game who turned out to be ordinary fans getting behind their team.

The same thing happens at skinhead gigs the world over. A chant of "Skinhead!" goes up, and nervous types immediately hear it as "Sieg heil!" and think a Nuremberg Rally choir has just started up.

A few short, sharp facts. Yes, there are skinheads with national socialist beliefs. No, not all skinheads hold national socialist beliefs – the majority do not. Being proud of your country and your heritage does not, by definition, make you a national socialist. Being a racist does not, by definition, make you a Nazi. Being pro-white does not, by definition, make you a racist. Being a skinhead does not, by definition, mean you are a Nazi, a racist, a patriot or anything else for that matter. Nearly all skinheads are patriotic. There's nothing wrong with being proud of your country. There will be those who do see it as a problem though because they say it can lead to racism, but if you applied that sort of logic to everything, walking down the street would be a crime – because you just might throw a brick through a window.

Obviously, skinheads have the right to support whatever political beliefs they want to – just like everyone else. The freedom to think and believe is something that nobody can take away from you, no matter how oppressive a regime you live under. Only that's not good enough for some people. Just because they believe in something strongly, they expect you to go along with it. They demand freedom of speech for themselves, but they want to silence you if you don't agree with them. And in their simplistic, blinkered, idealistic, arrogant little minds, everything is viewed in black and white, when anyone living in the real world will tell you there are also millions of shades of grey in between.

To dismiss people solely on one aspect of their life such as their political views – particularly when you are acting as both judge and jury – is not only arrogant and ignorant, but also very dangerous. You don't have to be a great fan of the extreme right to realise that until the politically correct hysteria and bullshit is removed from the debate, few people will be any the wiser.

The extreme right is always portrayed as being stupid, ignorant, and violent – and, of course, the word "Nazi" will be thrown in for good measure too. No doubt a few do live up to this stereotype (as do a few skinheads), but plenty more do not. The people behind Resistance Records may be a lot of things to a lot of people, but only an idiot would take them for mugs.

Not surprisingly, those who seriously advocate white supremacy and national socialism (and we're not talking about the WOGS OUT spray paint merchants here) don't see themselves as idiots. As they will tell you, it isn't ignorance that has led them to their views and beliefs, it is the pursuit of knowledge and truth that is often denied to the general public (cue conspiracy theories about the media being controlled by the Zionist Occupational Government – ZOG for short, the Holocaust being a hoax, and so on and so on).

White power music is also dismissed as being absolute rubbish by its detractors (and as with all music, some of it undoubtedly is). In his book, Skinhead Street Gangs, police officer and "nationally-recognised expert on skinhead gangs" Loren Christensen, described it as a "hard-driving, thumping, screaming, banging, thundering explosion of the most god-awful sounds this side of hell." If that really was the case with all white power music though, why do anti-fascist groups and the media go to such lengths to drive it underground? Why can't you walk into your local shop and find the latest Skrewdriver CD in the racks between The Skids and Slade?

"The media and trendy lefties want to promote black pride, gay pride, lesbian pride, and anything other than white pride. You're allowed to have a cop killer on TV programmes saying, yeah, buy my records, I'm a big black murderer, but you can't have someone saying these are my records, I sing about white pride, pride in my race, I don't hate anyone because of the colour of their skin, I'm just very proud of the skin colour I've got." So says Paul Burnley, lead singer of No Remorse, a skinhead of many years standing, and a national socialist.

After a spell as vocalist with Public Enemy (no relation to Chuck D's rap outfit you won't be surprised to hear), Paul went on to form No Remorse in the latter part of 1987. Together with the formation of Blood & Honour the same year, No Remorse heralded a new dawn for white power music and a far more extreme stance than had been taken before, at least publicly, as Paul himself explains.

"We said what we wanted to say without holding back anything. At the time, although it was a fairly big right-wing scene, some of the bands were saying they were are racist, but not that extreme. It all changed when Blood & Honour came into force, and after a while other bands were doing what we'd been doing from the beginning."

No Remorse's open and avowed Nazi stance allowed them to quickly establish a name for themselves in Blood & Honour circles. Even compared to Skrewdriver and Brutal Attack, they appeared to be far more extremist than anything that had gone before, particularly in Britain where victory over Hitler in World War Two has guaranteed a lack of enthusiasm for Nazism ever since.

Draped in swastika flags, the band's approach may have appeared basic and clumsy initially, but by 1990 and the release of the debut album, This Time The World (Rebelles European), No Remorse were one of the leading names on the Blood & Honour scene. Again, anyone concerned about censorship should ask themselves why you won't find No Remorse CDs in your local Our Price or Virgin Megastore. Plenty of other material that is offensive and controversial for a multitude of reasons does get carried. Nobody is forced to buy it.

It's really a question of freedom of speech, the right to say what you believe. It's well known that both the extreme left and the extreme right are as quick to demand it for themselves as they are to deny it to others, but no free society should allow self-appointed censors to dictate what you are allowed to listen to. If it's a matter of inciting racial hatred, then the law of the land should be brought into play.

"It's a great sadness that this society chooses to blacklist anyone they don't agree with", comments Paul, while talking about Ian Stuart and Skrewdriver. "Anybody, right-wing, left-wing, you should have the choice to listen to what you want, and you shouldn't be dictated to by middle class trendies in the music industry and over-zealous Zionists in the media. If his political views were so bad, why wasn't he free to say them and be exposed for it? The fact that he wasn't proves that he wasn't talking rubbish or spreading lies."

The Los Angeles riots that followed the not guilty verdict in the Rodney King police beating case saw Korean owned businesses singled out for looting and burning. Public Enemy's Chuck D has called it "precision bombing", black people hitting back at the Koreans who take money from the community, but give nothing back. Ice Cube has attacked Koreans for doing the same in his music. Both support Louis Farrakhan, the black separatist who is accused of being anti-Semitic and racist by the media. In fact, all three are condemned by the mainstream media, but they are still given the opportunity to state their case, they are given credit for other more positive aspects of their work, and the music of Ice Cube and Public Enemy is still widely available. So why treat white separatists and white power advocates any differently?

Personally, I don't have much time for white power music. Hard rock and thrash metal don't do much for me, and neither do the lyrics. I also don't believe there would be queues 'round the block to buy white power CDs if they were in the shops. In fact, the forbidden fruit appeal would disappear overnight.

Michael Jackson is one of the biggest names in the music business today. He recently performed at the Brit Awards, regularly appears on TV around the world and you can't turn the radio on without hearing one of his songs. This is the same man who was accused of sexually abusing children, but who paid millions of dollars to one alleged victim so that it would not to go court. To many people, those were not the actions of an innocent man, but walk into any record shop, and you can pick up his CDs by the dozen. That's disgraceful, but where's the outcry? Or is it just skinhead bands who have to adhere to the prevailing moral code?

Some will say that to allow racists to spread their message leads to racially-motivated violence, often with horrific consequences. The strange thing is the extreme right use the same argument against immigrants. Allow them into your country and it leads to muggings, drugs, and other crimes, again often with horrific consequences. Both statements contain a truth, but not the whole truth. Only a tiny minority of racists are involved in violence, just as only a tiny minority of immigrants are involved in crime.

There is no free debate in today's society. The extreme right, the Nazis, the white power merchants, the KKK, Tom Metzger, Resistance Records, No Remorse, they are all evil, bad, sinister and they've got it wrong. End of story. No questions asked. No platform for Nazis. Smash the National Front. And in place of free debate, we have media hysteria and related nonsense. The British National Party wants to hold a rally in a town hall and all hell breaks loose. Pickets, student marches, end of the world doom merchants. 100 drug related deaths in the city of Glasgow alone during 1995, thousands more caught up in a seedy world of crime, prostitution, poverty and violence to pay for their addiction. Where are the placard wavers? Where are the marches against the drug dealers and pushers? They are a far bigger threat to daily life than the extreme right will ever be, so why no Anti-Drug League?

In Moss Side, Manchester, drug wars have escalated into gun warfare on the streets. Every month or so, a small item on the news will tell you another person has been shot dead. Often they are just innocents, caught in the crossfire. Another murder. Another death too many. But why aren't the same people who flood the streets to protest about a racially-motivated killing out on the streets against the drug barons? Is one death more important than the other? Obviously so, at least to those who see racism as the ultimate evil. If all things were equal, the streets would be jam-packed after both events. Political correctness dictates differently.

It's impossible to say what percentage of skinheads support Blood & Honour and related organisations. If you only attend white power concerts, only kick about with like-minded skins, and only read white power literature, then the chances are you believe that the vast majority of skinheads are like yourself.

"Most skinheads are right-wing," argues Paul Burnley. "Possibly they aren't right-wing when they become skinheads, but they become right-wing because they are in a position to see things as other people don't. I think the right-wing is growing at the moment, particularly in Scandinavia, Germany, USA and other places where there is a steady flow of people getting off their backsides and not leaving it to anyone else. These are young people taking the initiative to promote the things they want to see. In the past, the skinhead thing has been controlled by older people who maybe weren't interested in anything other than making a profit, but now we can make our own CDs and produce our own records and things like that."

Obviously, a skinhead with no interest in the extreme right who goes to reggae and Oi! gigs with other skins just interested in having a beer and a laugh without the soap box politics will tell you different. In their world, most skinheads aren't right-wing.

The reality probably isn't far away from 40-60% of the world skinhead population being supporters of what can broadly be labelled the extreme right. Whether they really are the majority is hard to say because it stands to reason that 40-60% of skinheads don't support those views. Of those who don't though, only around 5-10% are staunchly anti-racist (as opposed to non-racist) and support SHARP or similar organisations. It also has to be said that a fair number of right-wing skinheads only become skinheads to outwardly express their racist beliefs and have no real love of the cult beyond that.

The media's constant focus on the sensational aspects of the skinhead cult, be it politics or violence or whatever, inevitably gives the impression that all skinheads are the same. Thick fascist thugs. This drip effect has been non-stop since the first skinheads laced up their boots and walked out onto the streets in the late Sixties, and the damaged caused to the cult is now beyond repair.

Skinheads, of course, aren't boy scouts. Most couldn't care less what the media or anyone else thinks about them. You certainly don't become a skinhead to win popularity contests. But constant media bullshit has created a situation where skinheads, together with football hooligans, new age travellers, single mothers, and other tabloid targets, are the new minorities who can be attacked at will, regardless of the true facts.

There is obviously good and bad in every race, creed and colour, and minorities deserve to be protected from persecution of any kind, but when skinheads are wronged in the media, there are no pressure groups to stand up for their rights. Nobody shouts foul. Nobody gives a fuck, to be honest.

During 1993, it seemed that you couldn't turn on the TV in Britain without being confronted by one drama series or another touting episodes about Nazi skinheads. They were queuing up to pay script writers vast sums of money to come up with the same old tired story line. Between The Lines, a drama series that deals with corruption within the police force, was a main part of the BBC's Autumn schedule. A trailer for the episode on police infiltration of a racist gang featured a skinhead doing press ups in front of a poster featuring skinheads with the words RACE IS OUR RELIGION above their heads. Pretty standard fair you would think, but the poster actually featured clearly identifiable Glasgow skinheads dancing away at a Laurel Aitken gig. Apparently, when a poster of Nazi skinheads could not be found, someone at the BBC thought any poster of skinheads would be fine once the racist slogan had been added. There was nothing to suggest the skinheads had any racist connection, and of course they did not, but that didn't seem to bother anyone until complaints were made.

The programme's producer, Peter Norris, was at first reluctant to edit the scene. After all, he had consulted the anti-fascist magazine Searchlight (a publication that rightly berates newspapers for its sensationalist approach to stories about immigration, black crime, and the like, but regularly publishes skinhead-related material itself that is no better researched). Mr. Morris also thought that the fact that the poster only appeared on screen for 15 seconds meant that it would cause few problems. However, when it was pointed out that he wouldn't have been too pleased to see his face on TV for 15 seconds with the words CHILD MOLESTER or MUGGER above it, he agreed that a mistake had been made. In the end, the programme was edited and the trailer not repeated, but you can guarantee few other minority groups would have been used and abused in this way in the first place.

On Saturday, October 1st, 1994, No Remorse, Nordic Thunder, and other white power bands had gathered in Wisconsin to hold a tribute concert for Ian Stuart. After the concert, at approximately 2:15am, a number of skinheads went into a local convenience store to buy food and beer to take to a party that had been arranged. Inside the shop, an argument broke out between the skinheads and three black youths who then left the shop unharmed.

One returned minutes later with a gun, presumably taken from a car parked outside, and he opened fire on the skinheads. The lead singer of Nordic Thunder, "Hammer" Joe Rowan, was hit and died almost immediately. To his friends and comrades within the white power movement, a great crime had been committed. The Church Of The Creator doctrine states that if any member of its church is murdered, then ten revenge killings must be committed against the enemy. The fact that nobody has been charged for the murder, despite the gunman being positively identified, has added insult to fatal injury.

Some people reading this no doubt couldn't care less whether a Nazi gets killed or not. For skinheads, white power or otherwise, this story underlines a deeper problem though. If it had been a group of skinheads with no political affiliations in that store, and an argument had broken out resulting in a skinhead being shot dead, people would have drawn the same conclusions. Race must have been an issue because skinheads were involved, and the skinheads probably started the trouble anyway and got what they deserved.

In Detroit, there are white power skinheads, but there are also skins in the city who are not white power. There are even skinheads in Detroit who aren't even white. Thanks to the media, the general hysteria surrounding extreme right-wing politics, the lack of any reasoned debate and the ignorance of those who seek to destroy the skinhead cult, the general public is unlikely to be aware of that fact.

No wonder a favourite skinhead tattoo reads, PERSECUTED BY MANY, UNDERSTOOD BY FEW.

Neither Red Nor Racist

The kids they come from everywhere, the East End's all around, claimed the back cover of the Carry On Oi! LP (Secret). Never was a truer word spoken, and as far as the skinhead cult is concerned, it's more applicable to the cult today than it has ever been.

Few people are surprised that there are still skins in the UK and Ireland, or even countries like Australia, New Zealand, and South Africa because of their long-standing connections with the motherland. The media has seen to it that virtually everyone is aware that there are also skinheads in Germany, Eastern Europe, and the USA, but that really is the tip of the skinhead iceberg. In fact, the skinhead cult must represent one of Britain's most successful exports in recent years.

Prior to shutting up shop in early 1995, Skinhead Times had subscribers in 44 countries. As well as readers in every Western European country, much of Eastern Europe including Russia and other former Soviet states, and North America, copies of the quarterly newspaper that covered skinhead news, street music and sport (mainly combat sports and football aggro) also found their way to far-flung countries like Argentina, Brazil, Chile, Colombia, Israel, Japan, Malaysia, Mexico, The Philippines, Singapore, and Zimbabwe. Maybe surprising to outsiders, but some of these countries are well known to other skins as homes of large skinhead communities – Brazil for example, can count its "carecas" in thousands, while Japan boasts as many Oi! bands as the UK does these days.

When you actually sit down and think about it though, it's quite incredible that what must be the most British of youth cults has now been adopted by kids the world over. The British Embassy staff in Manila must have thought they had had one gin and tonic too many when it was discovered that skinheads had sprayed DON'T PAY THE POLL TAX on the building that houses them. Even when you think of closer to home, and the richer countries of Europe, it's difficult to imagine the bovver brigade at home in the streets of Milan, Paris, and Geneva, but that's exactly where you will find them.

Oslo in Norway is one of the most expensive cities in the world – a hamburger, chips, and a can of coke cost around £10. It looks a prosperous city too and is one of only a handful of countries where the royal family can ride about on bicycles without any real problems. It is home to around half a million people and not surprisingly a few of them just happen to be skinheads.

"I first became a skinhead ten years ago mainly because of the music and because I didn't want to be like everyone else," says Kjetil, who as well as being one of Oslo's longest serving skinheads is also front man of street punk band, The Fuck Ups. "In the early Eighties, there were some skins in Oslo, but it was basically punks shaving their heads because they were into Oi! music. There wasn't many. It wasn't until about '86 that real skins started to show up in Oslo, me and some friends, three or four of us."

Another one of the first skinheads in Oslo now fronts the city's other street punk band, The Whalers – so called to annoy those who protested when Norway decided to resume whaling in 1992, and not in honour of Bob Marley's band.

"I first became a skinhead in 1987. I had always been listening to 2 Tone and Oi!, but I used to be a punk, but then it became too involved in politics. I didn't know much about the skinhead cult as there weren't any skinheads in Oslo. When I became a skinhead, I was the second one so there were only two! We didn't know too much, but we knew what skinheads looked like and we knew the music, and then we met some skinheads from Sweden and got some fanzines to keep updated."

Within a year or so, a handful of others had joined the ranks of the Oslo Skins and by 1990 there were around 20-30 in the city. It was in that year that SHARP – Skinheads Against Racial Prejudice – first came to the city too.

"This bonehead leader came to Oslo and tried to recruit from our skinhead scene," remembers Kalle who first became a skinhead in '89, "and we felt that we didn't want to have anything to do with this Nazi. Norwegians, they don't like Nazis. We were occupied by the Nazis during the war and feel they should be kept away. So we made this SHARP patch and we told our friends, you wear this patch or you fuck off."

It wasn't until 1991 that racist skinheads, known as the Boot Boys or Norwegian Skins, started to appear regularly in Oslo. Initially, they were more into drinking than politics and there was little division between the two gangs. That summer saw the first outbreaks of trouble, but any remaining links were severed that September. The Boot Boys had been on a Nazi demonstration which had ended in violence, and the media were falling over themselves to give coverage to the Nazi skins. To add a measure of balance to the coverage, members of SHARP-Oslo went to the media to let it be known that not all skinheads were racist, and some positive coverage followed. One of the interviews featured Kalle and Erik, and in it Erik made it clear that Nazi boneheads would not be welcomed in Oslo's Old Town, the part of the city (the East End naturally enough) where most of the SHARP skins lived.

To the Oslo Skins, SHARP was "just a badge, just a statement against the growing Nazi scene," as Marin, one of only two skingirls in the city explained. The media could only see things in strictly political terms though, and assumed that SHARP must be left-wing.

Just to make sure a Communist newspaper understood exactly what the score was, Erik bought a SMASH COMMUNISM t-shirt especially for an interview and was pictured wearing it, standing beneath the SHARP Oslo logo.

"Because of all the Nazi skin bullshit in the media, several skins in and around Oslo contacted us to join us," Kalle said, "because they knew we weren't racists or commies and because we kept the traditional skinhead style alive. All the skins in our SHARP section are 100% skinhead, and we don't allow non-skinheads to wear it. Even punks who maybe look like skins don't get the button. Loads of people have asked to join us just because they have short hair and maybe a bomber jacket, but we told them SHARP is for skinheads to show they are not Nazis, and not for punks to show they are not Nazi skins."

A month or so after the media attention, The Boot Boys fanzine carried an article on SHARP saying that they had to be "crushed once and for all". Addresses of SHARP skins were given as were details of a pub used by them. Following this came an interview in Norway's biggest newspaper in which the leader of The Boot Boys, a Nazi called Ole who had done time for throwing bombs, repeated threats against the SHARP crew.

November came and the SHARP skins heard rumours that a large gang of Boot Boys had attacked anti-fascists who had been leafleting in the city centre. That evening, a pub used regularly by the SHARP skins was attacked, but at the time there were only punks inside. Later that evening, a 30 strong mob of SHARP skins and punks went looking for the Boot Boys, but only managed to find Ole and another bonehead at the railway station – both (together with a have a go hero who tried to help them) ended up in hospital, and soon afterwards Ole lost interest in politics.

The trouble spilled over into 1992, with rumours that The Boot Boys were to call on VAM skins from neighbouring Sweden as reinforcements in their war against the Oslo SHARP skins, but there has been little serious trouble between the two factions since (Sweden is home to a very well-organised and growing white power movement, with VAM standing for Vitt Ariskt Motständ – White Aryan Resistance in Swedish).

Today, the skinhead scene is still firmly divided between white power skinheads who number around 150 and tend to come from outside of Oslo, and skinheads with no interest in extreme right wing politics, who number around 50 and are largely concentrated in Oslo and the port town of Stavanger.

"The really big gap is between the right-wing skinheads and everybody else and then there are small gaps between the other groups, but we don't fight each other," explains Erik, who no longer wears the SHARP patch and sees himself now as "a skinhead, plain and simple".

Mats, another Oslo skinhead, agrees. "Most people in Oslo are aware that the Oslo Skins aren't fascists. There are fascist skins in Oslo, but they are all cowards. They won't dare show their faces in the streets unless there are at least 20 of them. Our scene is not so divided. Unpolitical skins, SHARP skins and the few who are red skins all go to concerts together and hang out together, but we don't mix with racist skins."

This divide can be found more or less the world over, with the white power scene leading a largely separate existence from the rest of the skinhead scene. Occasionally you come across skinheads who embrace all aspects of the scene and are as happy to watch No Remorse as they are to find an old Trojan single, and in some places racist skinheads and non-political skins will be part of the same scene, but that is increasingly the exception rather than the rule.

Like Erik and a number of other skins, Mats no longer supports SHARP. "I started out as a SHARP skin in '90-'91, but a few years ago I got bored with the whole SHARP thing. It became more and more political so I took off the badge."

Kjetil, one of the first to call himself a SHARP skin also no longer supports it. "The reason I thought SHARP was good was because I personally wanted to show people that I wasn't a racist. But after a while, we started getting a lot of shit because people thought it was a group fighting against fascism and so I quit. I've got better things to do than spend my time fighting Nazis. In Oslo, we've got no Nazi skins, or at least you never see them. We have SHARP skinheads and your normal skinheads, but we all stick together because there aren't that many of us and we're all old friends."

Others continue to wear their SHARP patch though. "For me it's different," explains Thomas, another skinhead convert from the Norway punk scene. "To me, SHARP has never been a political group. I have never discussed politics with any of my SHARP friends. If a person comes up to me and asks me if I'm a SHARP skin, I still say yes."

"Politics shouldn't have anything to do with the cult, but when the media says all skins are Nazis, you have to take a stand against that," argues Marin. "The Nazi skinheads see us as very political just as we see them as very political, but it all gets coloured by the media."

True enough, SHARP is seen by white power skins as their opposite number on the skinhead scale, and of course the media, never slow at jumping to conclusions, naturally places SHARP on the left of the political spectrum. In some places, SHARP has been bastardised to resemble a politically-motivated anti-racist organisation, but that's not what SHARP was originally intended to be. Initially,

SHARP had no place on the political spectrum whatsoever. It was a simple statement that not all skinheads were racists. Full stop.

"Politics fucks the skinhead cult up," says Kalle. "There's nobody into ideologies or stuff like that in SHARP Oslo. If that comes in, then people can sit there having discussions about Marx or Hitler and it's just bollocks."

"When you do an interview, you want to talk about style, you want to talk about football, beer, going out with friends and all that," adds Thomas. "But the problem is, the media just wants to know, 'Which side are you on?'. There's always going to be a Nazi on the next page so it sets up the divide again."

It is very wrong that the Oslo Skins, and skinheads the world over, have been driven to the point where they are continuously asked to take sides in a political debate many just aren't interested in. No other youth cult is subjected to the same bullshit. The sensationalist aspect of the media is partly to blame for always seeking to define skinheads as political foot soldiers of one army or another. The extreme right-wing also shares some of the blame for targeting the skinhead cult, aided and abetted by its number one recruitment tool, the mainstream media. The left-wing is no better because sections of it are only too happy to keep the 'all skinheads are Nazis myth' alive because it suits them better than the truth.

And of course, some skinheads are to blame too for acting out the media stereotype and for allowing their own political views to infringe on the traditions of the skinhead cult. It's got to the point where skinheads, who have never been looking for society's blessing anyway, don't see why they should have to keep explaining themselves when they would get more response banging their heads against brick walls.

"You can sit down with people for three or four hours and tell them you're not a racist, tell them the history of skinheads from the Sixties and all that stuff," Kjetil sighs, "and still they think you're a Nazi."

In fact, the role of SHARP, politics and media bullshit play only a small part in the lives of the Oslo Skins. Just as with skinheads the world over, life mainly revolves around style, drinking, gigs, drinking, football, drinking, aggro, and, er, more drinking. Style-wise, nearly all of the Oslo skinheads dress smartly. In fact, it is perhaps the only way the general public can tell them apart from racist skinheads in Norway, very few of whom dress traditionally in skinhead terms (not that the general public sees anything beyond shaved heads and boots anyway).

Another small distinction between the two camps is that white power skins tend to wear a Norwegian flag patch on their jackets, while the Oslo Skins don't – although the Norwegian flag will appear on their football scarves and so on.

"Nazis use the flag as a political statement," says Thomas, who could be talking about the Union Jack if he was British and not Norwegian. "They can't really walk around with swastikas and things like that, so they steal the Norwegian flag and use it."

Both The Fuck Ups and The Whalers gig regularly, as do Oslo ska band, MC Hammond (Skavenger is also home to another ska band, The Skanxters, and the Oslo crew regularly travel to see them). Even better, the Oslo Skins are fortunate enough to drink at a pub that has its own upstairs function room complete with bar and stage. When we visited the city to film for World Of Skinhead, a gig was arranged with just a day's notice, allowing us to see for ourselves that The Fuck Ups really are one of the best street punk bands of today as hinted at by their debut four track EP, Al's My Pal (Jala Records and Knock Out Records). What's more, The Whalers were well worth seeing too, with their hard driving Oi! sound going down well with the decent size crowd.

For the Oslo Skins, it was a near perfect night. Norway beating Luxemburg live on TV in the downstairs bar followed by a gig upstairs, and then by an early morning visit to the Pitbull Club (for those who didn't have work in the morning and for those who did have work, but who were past caring). The Pitbull Club is actually a members only after hours drinking den and is frequented by the Oslo Skins and others from the city's alternative scene.

It's illegal, but the police turn a blind eye to it. It's the usual story of it being better to know where the skinheads are than close down the club and have them roaming the streets. It has a pool table, bar football, good music, and, of course, a well-stocked bar, but you know immediately that it's a haven for skinheads because of the large Clockwork Orange droog and 2 Tone man painted on the walls. The music coming out of the speakers – Oi!, punk, ska, skinhead reggae – gives a good indication to what the Oslo Skins listen to.

Before the Pitbull Club, the Oslo Skins had another place to call their own called Harry's Hangar. It was big enough for gigs and was also used as a gym for those into kick-boxing, a popular martial art amongst the Oslo Skins. Now with Harry's Hangar gone, they have managed to rent a room in an old factory building and this has been turned into a gym, complete with punch bags, speed ball, and partly mirrored walls.

"People just used to drink all the time, but as they get a little bit older, they want to stay in shape," explains Kalle. "For the last three years, a lot of people have been going to the gym to lift weights, and others have started Thai boxing, which is quite popular, and we have our own place where people can train."

And train they do too. The standard of work produced in the small gym is really good, as demonstrated by the height, quality, and accuracy of some of the kicks on display – the hardest part of any martial art to master. As well as for fitness, they train for street fights and because a number of the Oslo Skins work as bouncers in the city's nightclubs.

"A lot of people see a skinhead and want to fight you," says Thomas. "A lot of Oslo Skins work at nightclubs and you get people thinking, if I can beat a skinhead up I'll be a real man. So you get a lot of fights."

"We don't organise fights," adds Erik, "but they happen. Every year, we have an annual Oslo Skins Christmas Bash and at Christmas 1993, there were about 35 skinheads at a club drinking, and we left to get more beer. We went into a street with discos and fancy pubs and we started fighting with everyone. The bouncers in the street co-operate with each other and they all came to fight us. In the end, the coppers came and arrested ten of us."

Another opportunity for trouble comes with following Vålerenga, who are not only a football team, but have an ice hockey team too (complete with ice hockey hooligans). A lot of the Oslo Skins support Vålerenga and a club scarf is permanently on display in the Pitbull Club.

"I'm a little bit extreme," says Kalle. "Violence can be fun sometimes, it gives you adrenaline rushes, but most of us don't use blind violence. It's just that we don't take shit from anyone. So sometimes, it's fighting in the town centre at weekends. People come to hassle you because you're a skinhead. They don't care if you are a Nazi, anti-Nazi or whatever you are. They keep bothering you so it comes to a fight. Lots of people, the only language they understand is violence. Like if a big guy wants to fuck you up, you can't just sit there and talk to him. He'll just laugh at you and you'll lose face. Violence is a way of getting respect."

There are arseholes the world over who think it's hard to have a go at skinheads, bikers, and similar gangs. If someone spills your beer it's bad enough, but in Oslo where each pint costs three times what it does in Glasgow, it takes on a whole new meaning. Not that all of the Oslo Skins see violence as the answer.

"Violence is fucking stupid," says Kjetil. "One day you'll get killed or kill somebody. It's okay to fight when you win, but one day you can't win and one day you get beaten up really bad, and I think that's the day people realise that violence isn't fun."

Partly because of the small size of Oslo and partly because of the close friendships that bond the Oslo Skins together, they have one of the best scenes to be found anywhere in Europe, and one that is more or less self-sufficient too. The only thing it lacks is enough skinhead girls.

"Most people don't see you as a skinhead because you have hair," says Marin, "and so think you must be a punk or just someone who hangs out with the boys. You are a little on the outside when you're a girl because you don't talk about the same things all the time or want to do the same things, and there's a comradeship between the gang and sometimes you feel on the outside. There are so few skingirls here and it's a very masculine cult."

One Law For Them

"Gangsta rap is black Oi!. That's the best comparison. It's the same working class ghetto mentality – against the world and fuck everybody." So says Lol Pryor, former manager of The Business, one time proprietor of Syndicate Records and Link Records, and currently the main man at Dojo Records. What's more, he's dead right too.

The similarities go well beyond the fact that both styles of music are, albeit to different degrees, frowned upon by the mainstream. The bands go under similar names, CD cover artwork captures the same street atmosphere, and lyrically, the same themes crop up – gangs, violence, police oppression, urban decay, pride in your own kind. A different style maybe and origins that are thousands of miles apart, but when all is said and done, gangsta rap and Oi! are the products of the same back streets. In fact, there are more than one or two gangbangers in Los Angeles who cruise around the city with Oi! music booming out of their car stereo system. And I kid you not.

The big difference is though that despite the fact that both have their critics, gangsta rap is far more acceptable to the likes of NME and Select than Oi! will ever be. The reason for this is as clear as day. Gangsta rap is viewed from a romantic distance – the closest these people get to L.A. violence is watching Colors on home video. Oi! music isn't like that though. It's just that little bit too real, that little bit closer to home. It's about the back streets of Britain where life has a nasty habit of slapping you one in the face.

From day one, Oi! has suffered from what could politely be called a public relations disaster. It's no compromise attitude won it a loyal army of followers, but at the same time alienated everyone else for miles around. Outsiders rarely took the time or trouble to find out what Oi! was all about and so relied on the often-repeated old faithfuls. Oi! is fascist rock. Oi! is crude, basic and worthless. Oi! is mindless noise. And so on and so on.

Greil Marcus, author of In The Fascist Bathroom ("A vital fin de siècle document" according to Rolling Stone magazine, "page after page of pretentious bullshit" according to me), dismissed Oi! as "1977 punk stripped of its humour and vision". I didn't realise the Pistols and the rest of the no future brigade had a vision, and as for humour, Joe Strummer was hardly up theere with the likes of Sid James and Charlie Chaplin. The funniest thing about '77 punk rock is the fact that the likes of Greil Marcus take it so bloody seriously.

"Someone once said that the original wave of punk rock had been about art school students jumping up and down and being naughty and upsetting daddy," recalls Lol Pryor. "I think Oi! really was about the kids coming in off the streets, out of the tower blocks and the building sites, and it was just for real. People say that Garry Bushell invented it, but all he did was write about 20 or 30 bands who were there, and that gave it a focal point. For a time it was called real punk or reality punk, but I think the Rejects' song, Oi! Oi! Oi! just summed it all up."

"I honestly believe we were the first and only band to walk it like we talked it," the Rejects' Micky Geggus claims, and with some justification. "I mean, nowadays with bands like Guns N' Roses, it's hip to be hard. It's how many tequilas you can drink and how many people you've bashed. In those days, we were blacklisted for doing what came naturally out of ignorance."

Garry Bushell was the journalist at Sounds who championed the street punk cause while everyone else in the same game was falling over themselves to find the next big thing now that 2 Tone was about to be dropped. Oi! had been around under various names since the early days of Cock Sparrer and Sham 69, and at least in attitude for a lot longer still.

"You can go back as far as The Small Faces, to be honest with you, for lads rock," argues Mr. Pryor, "but what really crystallised it after the punk thing must have been Sham, Cock Sparrer, The Rejects, Angelic Upstarts, even The Lurkers and Slaughter & The Dogs."

"Menace and them sort of bands were the harder edge of punk," adds Mark Brennan, former bass player with The Business and the founder of Link Records who now runs the collector's label, Captain Oi!. "They were the bands that I went to see and a lot of people I knew from those gigs then became The 4 Skins, Infa Riot, and so on."

Oi! was very much a continuation of punk, with each generation of bands inspiring the next generation. Members of The Cockney Rejects had been roadies with Sham, members of The 4 Skins had roadied for the Rejects and so it went on. Roi Pearce of The Last Resort and later of The 4 Skins was a roadie with Menace. And while all this was going on in London, street corner kids in other towns and cities were picking up guitars and forming bands too.

"1979, we started as a punk band doing Clash, UK Subs covers, things like that, and a mixture of our own songs," says Steve Smith, singer with Sunderland's Red Alert who are still gigging, still recording, and still knocking back too much beer to this day. "When the Eighties came around, we had heard Sham, then the Rejects came along and we just picked up on that. We all became skins over night. The Rejects got us into the Oi! thing and we just got carried along with it."

His brother, Patty, who is a member of another Sunderland street punk outfit, Red London, agrees. "Oi! is an extension of punk. When The Clash and the Pistols faded out, Oi! stepped in." And as if to underline this evolution, you only have to look as far as the B side of Sham 69's debut single, I Don't Wanna (Step Forward), to find the source of Red London's name.

Just as punk defined an attitude more than a style of music, the same was true of Oi! – something that will no doubt come as a big surprise to the "it all sounded the same" retards, but not to anyone who has actually heard any of the music.

"Oi! is having a laugh and having a say – simple as that," reckons Arthur Kay, bass player with The Last Resort. "It was good old street punk, punk without the pretension. It was kids in the streets strapping on guitars and giving it the big 'un."

Bands like The 4 Skins, Infa Riot, and The Last Resort represent the hardcore Oi! sound with terrace chants over in your face street punk tunes. The likes of The Business and The Crack offer a far more melodic but no less street sound, very much in the vein of Sparrer, a superb band who were given something of a second wind with Oi!. Then you had cross-over mohican and studs bands like The Exploited and Vice Squad, who from time to time threw their lot in with the charge of the Oi! brigade. And, of course, you had the madcap element in the shape of The Toy Dolls, Splodge, and others. And The Blood, one of the first bands to successfully bridge the punk-metal divide, were in there too with a depraved form of shock rock that really defies description (at least in a family publication such as this). Pat Gilbert was spot on in Record Collector when he wrote, "like most movements, Oi! was ultimately about a time, a place, and a bunch of kindred spirits."

To add to the confusion, not all of the bands associated with the music were happy with the Oi! tag. Blitz, who hailed from New Mills on the outskirts of Manchester and were in many ways the most successful of the Oi! bands, saw themselves as a straight-forward punk band. "Garry Bushell coined the phrase Oi!. We thought it segregated us from the rest of punk, when it's very difficult to say what the difference was between Oi! and punk. If there was one, I couldn't tell you what it is."

November 1st, 1980, and Oi! had made it onto the front cover of Sounds in the shape of 4 Skin, Garry Hodges. Oi! The Album (Sounds/EMI), a compilation of old and new street punk bands, including Cock Sparrer, the Cockney Rejects, the Angelic Upstarts, Slaughter & The Dogs, and The 4 Skins with Chaos and Wonderful World, came out the same month, and there was every reason to believe that Oi! would make it big time in 1981. A series of showcase gigs were organised in London at the start of the year, but two of the three gigs – the first one at Southgate, and the third one at Acklam Hall – ended in trouble.

The knockers were quick to condemn Oi! for encouraging a hooligan following, but the trouble was caused by outsiders on both occasions and it wasn't just Oi! gigs that were kicking off at the time. In fact Oi! gigs tended to be peaceful affairs.

"There was not the trouble at gigs people would have expected," says Nidge from Blitz. "If it did arrive, it was very small, the sort of thing you'd get at any gig."

The Oi! bandwagon continued to roll however, and the Strength Thru' Oi! compilation released on Decca in May made it to number 51 in the national charts. A number of large gigs were planned for that summer, but in the meantime a series of mini-festivals were organised which, in the words of promoter Dave Long, "would prove that Oi! is not about mindless violence." Unfortunately, one of the gigs just happened to be at the Hambrough Tavern in Southall.

"Before Southall, Oi! was obviously the next wave of punk that was going to take off," says Lol Pryor. "The 4 Skins had been offered a publishing deal, The Business had been offered a publishing deal, a lot of other big deals were being offered around, and Southall just buggered a lot of people up. A lot of people didn't really want to know the truth and just dropped it and went on to something else, whether it was new romantics or whatever it was at the time."

The gig at Southall featured The Business, The Last Resort, and The 4 Skins. Spirit Of '69 covers it in all its glory, so there's little point going over and over the same old ground. In a nutshell though, some minor disturbances before the gig involving local Asians and a handful of skinheads led to a full scale riot later that night, resulting in the gig being abandoned shortly before a hijacked police van was set on fire and rammed into the pub, setting it alight.

There was no doubt fault on both sides, but there was no need for the media or the politicians to find out what had really caused the riot – it was far more convenient to blame the Oi! bands and their skinhead following.

Lol was there with The Business that night. "With hindsight, people ask why was a gig held in Southall, but we'd played gigs in Lewisham, Deptford, Clapham, Stockwell, Hackney, and elsewhere in inner-London, so why shouldn't we play a gig anywhere else? Again with hindsight, certain people busing skinheads in on coaches with Union Jacks hanging out of windows wasn't really a clever idea, and the three or four skinheads who decided to go up the road and start on some Asians in a kebab shop didn't help the affair. But those skinheads were offered over to the police, but the police were reluctant to arrest them, and it got really out of hand. There's the funny stories like the PA man who chained the PA down because he was worried about skinheads, and then when the pub was burning down, he couldn't unchain his stuff fast enough. And The 4 Skins' manager chasing the pub manager up the road for his money even though the pub was burning down.

"There's the funny side to it and the bad side, but the stories that the press came out with – like skinheads were running out of the pub with petrol bombs… Well, as you know, every pub in England sells petrol bombs behind the bar. There were loads of reasons why it probably happened, but what later appeared in the media was nothing like what really happened."

Arthur Kay, who played with the Last Resort that night, agrees. "The Guardian was the only newspaper that gave both sides of the story. The tabloids gave a totally biased version and it was the end of Oi! as we knew it. It killed it. Bands like the Resort had to go underground. We couldn't play a gig in London because of the GLC so had to play under aliases."

The Southall riot put Oi! on the front pages of every newspaper in the country, but unfortunately for all the wrong reasons. It also saw the birth of myths that haunt Oi! to this day. As soon as journalists heard that the trouble was between Asians and skinheads, they didn't need to know anymore. Oi! is skinhead music, all skinheads are racist, Oi! is music for racists, skinheads cause trouble, blame the skinheads, end of story.

"Since the Southall riots, all skinheads have been branded Nazis by the media," complains Big Iain. "They are deaf to any other views. When I walk down the street, people will look at me and think, 'Nazi scum'. I know I'm not, my mates know I'm not, but to the normal Joe in the streets that's what I am. It's hard to walk about like this knowing people hate you while you still feel pride in what you are."

The Asian youths no doubt felt that they were justified in attacking the Hambrough Tavern that night, but whatever their reasoning, the fact remains that they caused the riot during the gig and continued to riot long after the gig was over. To suggest that the Oi! bands and their skinhead following were to blame, simply because of their very presence in Southall, is political correctness gone mad and gives credibility to a sensationalist media that it scarcely deserves. Would the same be said if a Moslem prayer meeting in a largely white area was petrol bombed by Christian white youths who found their presence inflammatory? And is it really such a crime to fly the Union Jack in the streets of Britain? Apparently so, if you are a white working class male.

"If you're upper class you can take the Union Jack to the last night of the Proms and you're a jolly good chap," argues Arthur Kay, "but if you fly the flag at a football match you're lower than a rattle snake's arse."

"Someone rang us up when we were running Link," recalls Mark Brennan, "and he'd counted all the Union Jacks on record covers and was convinced it was some sort of right wing conspiracy. Trainspotters Weekly stuff really."

Oi! was never just skinhead music either. It was for skins, punks, ex-mods, football casuals, herberts, anyone who cared to listen. Music for the football terraces. Just like with punk, the mod revival and 2 Tone before it, Oi!'s following was made up of mainly white kids, but it certainly wasn't exclusively white kids that supported Oi!. What's more, you are hard pressed to name an Oi! band that consisted of just skinheads back in '81. Not even The 4 Skins come close. Blitz were pure skunk – half-skin and half punk.

"We had two skinheads and two punks in the band," explains Nidge. "We were all listening to the same music, going to see the same bands, punks and skinheads all mixed in together. In the early days, there was trouble between punks and skinheads, but it started to come together more about that time, 1980-81. We got to realise we were all into the same thing so it became more unified."

In fact, if the truth be told, not all skinheads even liked Oi! music, and many thought it had nothing to do with the cult and its traditions, particularly when it picked up the gluebag following.

Brian Kelson - "The new breed of skinhead was born out of punk. The music was just like rock music, heavy metal rock music. The clothes were so scruffy; big boots, hair shaved right off. Totally different music, taking drugs, sniffing glue – no original skinhead would have done that, dossing like a hippy."

Today, it probably is true to say that most Oi! bands do consist of skinheads, and it's also the case that most of its fans are skinheads now too. But that's only because the music has received so much negative publicity that it has been left to the dedicated few to carry on flying the flag. It wouldn't take much though to blow it wide open again, and get a wider, more varied audience jumping around to the likes of Sweden's Agent Bulldogg, Italy's Klasse Kriminale, Germany's Voice Of Hate or England's Mr. Mighty Men.

As for Oi! being political, there seems little doubt in the minds of those involved with the music at the time.

"Absolutely not," says Lol Pryor. "You could always get hold of a skinhead from up north maybe who would say it was a left-wing movement, and somebody who was walking along the road outside Chelsea football ground – and I use that because the media loves to pick on them – who would say it was a right-wing thing. I don't think it ever was. There were people who had been involved in politics and if you ever get any working class movement of any sort, you're going to get people who are involved in politics, be they left or right. These people had been involved, but I don't think any of the bands had ever written anything political other than anti-Establishment."

Mark Brennan agrees. "If there was any politics, it was street politics, politics with a small P, not party political nonsense. Things that concerned ordinary people from whatever area, whether it's The Partisans from Wales or The Business from Lewisham. We did Sabotage The Hunt, but nobody picks up on that and says that's a political song, but it was. Nobody picks up on Employer's Blacklist. Last Train To Clapham Junction was about nuclear waste going through London. That affects everyone. Left, right, black, white. Oi! was the politics of life. It was more concerned about local issues, not The Clash singing about the Sardinistas. It was more on the ball. More realistic than idealistic."

Again, as with skinheads, nobody is really interested in what Oi! stands for as long as they can label it as fascist rock. Until Matty smacked a Melody Maker journalist, The Blaggers ITA were the darlings of the music press because of their outspoken stance against fascism. When they signed to a major record label, they spent money that would have been used for throwing release parties for music business saps on full page ads in the music press, urging others to stand firm against racism. As any skinhead will tell you, The Blaggers started life as a fully fledged Oi! band, with House Of The Fascist Scum appearing on their debut album, On Your Toez (Oi! Records), so it's as obvious as a kick in the balls that Oi! isn't by definition racist.

"The Oi! thing was more of an attitude," reckons Watford Jon, who now finds himself in Oi! band Argy Bargy after being a fan of the music for many years. "It was that stand up for yourself, believe in yourself, fight for yourself attitude, and as long as people have got the hump with the way they're always told to do things, you'll always have some form of Oi! music."

There's no getting away from the fact that part of Oi!'s support came from skinheads and others who were right-wing – the same was true for 2 Tone, such were the times – but Oi! also had support from the left wing and from people with no interest in politics whatsoever. It's a total fallacy that Oi! was racist rock.

"We made it clear in songs like Propaganda that we absolutely weren't right-wing," explains Nidge, "and we did the same through the interviews we did, so we never had a fascist element turning up at gigs."

Outsiders who claim Oi! is racist music usually cite bands like Skrewdriver as examples, but as Ian Stuart said in an interview for Spirit Of '69 back in 1991, "We've never been an Oi! band. I would say we were a rock band."

No Remorse's Paul Burnley agrees. "It's rock music really. It's hard to define because No Remorse is different from a lot of bands, but we strive to be more Seventies style rock than heavy metal, thrashing guitars and stuff. We're striving for the music to be powerful, but not to drown out the lyrical content. We're not an Oi! band. We never really associated ourselves with the Oi! thing, although our music was very similar in the beginning to Oi! and skinhead punk music."

Southall should have spelled the end of Oi!. It certainly stunted its growth for a short time – gigs were cancelled, shops refused to stock Oi! releases, and the mainstream music industry couldn't distance itself quick enough.

"A lot of people begrudgingly went into Oi!," says Mark Brennan, "no different to how they begrudgingly went into picking up rap bands a year later. Industry-wise, nobody really liked it in the first place, but it was happening, they had to do something with it, and then Southall came along and it was all – 'Told you' – and that's it. Knock it on the head and leave it. Whereas, things have happened since where people have been killed – nobody was killed at Southall – and they still fall over themselves to get their cheque books out."

In fact, just ten days after Southall, a black teenager was stabbed to death at a gig at the Rainbow Theatre in London. If it had happened at an Oi! gig, you can bet your life that the moral majority would have been jumping up and down, calling for Oi! to be banned, but seeing as it was at a concert by roots reggae band Black Uhuru, it was quickly forgotten. Hardly surprisingly, the Oi! bands felt they had been treated unjustly over Southall, a sentiment echoed on The 4 Skins' debut single on their own Clockwork Fun label, One Law For Them.

They might have been down, but against all the odds Oi! was quickly to prove it was far from beaten. Carry On Oi! was released that October on Secret Records, and found its way to number 60 in the national charts. Amongst others, the album was dedicated to Martin Luther King, and Khalid Kharim and the Pakistani Punks and Skins. Other bands released singles, although big sales by the likes of The 4 Skins suspiciously didn't result in chart placings.

"If you look at the sales the bands were doing just before and after Southall, and compare it to what Carter and Manic Street Preachers do now, it was obvious Oi! should have charted at the time," says Lol Pryor. "The first Business single did about 35,000 in the UK, The Blitz album did 40,000 in the UK with no promotion, no TV, no radio. That's quite incredible really."

Blitz's debut album, Voice Of A Generation, was actually a top 30 hit, and underlines the generally held belief that they were the most successful of the Oi! generation. Like the others though, they had no great aspirations to conquer the world.

"We saw an advertisement in Sounds for a new record label advertising for bands," says Nidge of the band's introduction to the No Future record label. "We sent them the four tracks we'd recorded at our own expense, and they said they'd release it as a single. They just pressed 1,000 copies, and we thought it would be great if we could sell them, and it ended up selling 25,000 copies so it was a big surprise. Suddenly, coming from nowhere to number two in the independent charts."

For a year or so after Southall, the Oi! flag continued to fly proudly with little in the way of trouble. In fact, the biggest danger to the general public seemed to be if you were unfortunate enough to be on the same stretch of motorway as Red Alert's hired van.

"We drove down to London in a big Luton van for a gig once, with 20 skinheads in the back, three lads in the front," remembers Steve Smith. "And everybody was that drunk, it ended up with about ten different people having a go at driving the van. We were all young kids, 18 and 19, with one licence between us, and this happened going and coming back. And the van was all over the road, up on the grass verge…"

Oi! though had given up any hope of making it to the centre stage again, and one by one bands began to call it a day. When Syndicate released the Oi! Of Sex compilation in 1984, things had reached such a low point that a number of the bands including Prole, Crossed Hammers, and The Orgasm Guerillas were little more than studio bands dreamed up to help fill up the album. Label boss Ron Rouman explained the situation in the sleeve notes for the 1994 CD re-release of the album on the Captain Oi! label.

"Although we were getting tapes in from new bands, most of them were crap and so rather than have a so-so Oi! compilation, we felt it better to alter things a little so that we got a great Oi! LP to help keep the scene alive. It must also be said that of all the bands on Syndicate, the one we received the most mail for was Prole and we were actually going to do a Prole LP."

Sadly, Syndicate weren't long for this world, but the flame continued to flicker throughout the Eighties until first Oi! Records and then Link Records once again gave the music a whole new lease of life. Link especially, with its extensive re-issue programme and breaking of new talent, laid the foundations for today's Oi! scene that has spread throughout the world. And nowhere is that truer than the United States Of America.

The 1995 release, Backstreets Of American Oi! – Unreleased Anthems (Sta Press Records), contained tracks from no fewer than 25 bands from all over North America. Bands like The Anti-Heroes from Atlanta, Georgia, Boot Party from Fresno, California, and Sons Of Pride from Brossard in Quebec, Canada. And there will be other bands who didn't make it onto this particular release, but who will turn up elsewhere. As the sleeve notes say, "It is true that the English set the pace for street rock-n-roll, and that classic bands such as Last Resort, Cock Sparrer, 4-Skins, and the like are often imitated but will never be duplicated. England will always be respected for the introduction of Oi!. However, the time has come for the whole world to see who's leading the race…"

In terms of quantity, the above's no doubt true, but in terms of quality, only the top flight of U.S. Oi! bands come close to the standards set by their British counterparts. What's more, a few of the American bands are really doing nothing more than playing Oi! by numbers, giving rise to the view that they are little more than second rate Last Resort wannabes. Even so, there are still at least a handful of Oi! bands in the States with the potential to produce music that could rival the very best street rock n' roll sounds. It's such a fresh, young and exciting scene, you can believe anything is possible.

One massive advantage American Oi! has over its British cousin is that it doesn't have a Southall to continually justify. And given the multi-racial nature of the U.S. scene and the fact that the white power scene is totally detached from it, it's never likely to have either.

"There's always been black people into it over here," says Perry from Chicago, who is himself involved in a couple of Oi! bands at present, The Templars and Chapter 21. "I've always seen black skinheads over here, so to us it's really no big deal."

Interestingly enough, when media hysteria about Nazi skinheads was at its peak, the reality of the cult at street level was so different, that more non-whites were turning skinhead than ever before. Even so, you still get mugs who see that skinheads are involved and assume it's some kind of fascist rock.

A young lady by the name of Laura runs a community radio show in Windsor, Canada, which, thanks to a quirk in geography, actually lies to the south of Detroit in the States. Although not a skingirl, she gives plenty of support to skinhead bands, with her playlist consisting almost exclusively of Oi!, punk and early American hardcore. "I've been called sexist, anti-female, definitely considered racist, fascist, right-wing – and I'm careful what I play! I don't want to play anything political, I'm not political myself, and I think it's just because people hear the word skinhead in a song and think, 'Oh, this person's a neo-Nazi'. That's a minority though – most feedback is positive."

The UK still seems to be able to come up with the goods musically, even if the bands are forced to go to Europe and even America to get anything close to recognition for their efforts. Recent losses like Another Man's Poison and Pressure 28, two bands who led something of a new breed of Oi! in the early Nineties, are sorely missed, but there are still the likes of Blank Generation in Wycombe, Braindance in Norwich, and Boisterous and Crashed Out flying the Oi! flag in the North East.

A lot of the British Oi! bands and their following consist of skinheads who have been around since the early Eighties and who refuse to throw in the towel. The fact remains that very little new blood is coming into the cult in Britain these days, and the same is true of Oi!, and yet against all the odds, Hebburn in the North East throws up Crashed Out, an Oi! band made up of school mates. What's more, they have managed to build up a decent size skinhead crew centred around a love of Oi!, boxing, and the band.

Lee, who also plays with Cramlington-based Boisterous, followed in his brother Colin's footsteps as far as discovering the joys of Oi! and boxing are concerned. Colin had also been a skinhead, so it was not too surprising he followed suit there too. After passing some cassette tapes of classic Oi! around at school and the boxing gym, more and more of his mates got into it, shaved their heads and a new generation of Hebburn Skins was born.

"Pop music is just crap," says Lee. "Oi! is true life music, that's what we're in it for. It's about things that really happen in the streets and it's by ordinary people, not pop stars that you can't talk to."

Cein, another Hebburn Skin, agrees. "Pop songs are all about love and happy endings, but that doesn't happen in real life all the time, does it? What's so good about doing three chords on a keyboard and repeating it over and over again? That's all it is really. Oi! music is about things that really happen."

What's really amazing about the Hebburn Skins is that they didn't follow the vast majority of today's kids into the dance scene.

"I hate rave and all that music," Lee explains. "It's just crap. All it does is advertise drugs all the time – that's all it ever goes on about. There's just no point to it. Our music has got a point. It's about real life, kids on the street, so why shouldn't they listen to it? All the gangs are just raving, rappers, and it's a load of crap. They should shave their hair and listen to our kind of music. It's about everything they do on the street. All you rave kids with pants hanging off your arses, take a look in the mirror and then take a look at us. This is the real world."

The current success of hardcore punk bands like Green Day, Rancid, and Offspring (Offspring alone have notched up sales of over seven million CDs as of 1996) looks like it may spill over onto the Oi! scene. These bands were listening to Oi! music as kids and they aren't ashamed to admit it. Rancid have been on MTV saying that Oi! is working class protest music and nothing else, and have regularly finished live sets with a cover of Blitz's Someone's Gonna Die Tonight. And in true street music fashion, labels like Epitaph are run by true fans of the music. The Business who are currently touring the States for the second time regularly team up with hardcore punk bands for shows, especially their good friends, Madball, so the cross-over is already happening.

All it is going to take is one band to breakthrough into the big time, and Oi! still has every chance of surpassing anything it has achieved to date. The talent's most certainly there, and all they're waiting for is the first glimmer of an opening and they'll be straight in there.

Oi! is generally written off in most mainstream circles, but it has outlasted most of the so-called big acts that were around at the time Oi! first kicked its way onto the music scene.

"A Haircut 100 single is worth tuppence today, while the 4 Skins first single is worth £15," says Ron Rouman. "That's a testimony to what it was all about."

His close associate Lol Pryor naturally agrees. "When we started Link Records we were told by one of the largest distributors that we wouldn't last three releases, and we lasted 300 before we wanted to do something different."

The school of '81 have inspired a world-wide explosion of Oi! bands who can now be found all over North and South America, Europe, Australia, and elsewhere. The critics can knock it all they like, but one thing is for certain. Oi! music is going to be around to get right up their noses for many years to come.

"Oi! is working class music," says Steve Smith. "Beer-drinking music. It's a street level thing and there's a real bond there. The media hates us, but we don't care. The opposition to Oi! makes it stronger, and that drives us on."

Tougher Than Tough

"1974, Manchester United against Manchester City at Old Trafford, Dennis Law accidentally scored the goal which more or less put United into the Second Division." Doing the talking is Nidge Miller, founding member of Blitz and one time member of Man. Utd's infamous Red Army. In his hands is a perfectly kept scrapbook of neatly folded newspaper cuttings and the double page spread he's looking at shows scenes of crowd trouble and pitch invasions, with the headline, THE FINAL HEARTBREAK. "I wouldn't say I was responsible really. I just jumped onto the pitch and 10,000 people followed me! And that put a stop to the game basically!"

Nobody who grew up in the Seventies hasn't heard of the Red Army. It invaded the towns and cities that United were playing in, and went on the rampage before, during, and after the match. Some of the fans were on the pitch more often than Georgie Best.

This continued for most of 1974 and 1975 as football hooliganism reached new heights, resulting in the introduction of crowd segregation. But, for a time, it seemed that the government ran the country six days of the week, and Saturday belonged to the Red Army. The press called the Red Army animals, and a new terrace chant was born at Old Trafford – "WE HATE HUMANS!"

"To try and give you an idea of the number of skinheads then, just a small town like New Mills with a population of 10,000, you'd see a crowd of 50 skinheads and bootboys going down to see Manchester United, and now you'd be lucky to find 50 in the whole of the city of Manchester. In the Stretford End itself, there were literally thousands of bootboys."

The late Sixties and early Seventies were the golden era for those involved in mass football violence in Britain. Skinheads had been the first youths to really take over the terraces and travel to away games. The lack of crowd segregation at the time meant that it was inevitable trouble would kick off every time emotions ran high, and the aggro soon became as big an attraction as the game itself.

Moon Records' supremo, Rob Hingley, was a Plymouth Argyle fan at the time. "On a Saturday you'd get dressed up, get the bus down to Plymouth to watch Argyle get mauled, try to get into the pubs, get thrown out, get beat up by the opposing teams' skinheads. There was always more of them and they were always older than you. Don't know how that happened, but it was always the case. Going down and getting bounced around on a Saturday afternoon at Plymouth – good times!"

"Around '70-'71, when you used to go down to Roker Park to see Sunderland play, three quarters of the crowd were skinheads," remembers Gaz Stoker, and the like was to be found at both English and Scottish football grounds around the country. "It looked brilliant. It was the first fashion you got into and was something to belong to. Brilliant stuff."

As skinhead progressed into suedehead and then into bootboy, football hooliganism remained a constant theme.

"When I was about 14, I went to a Chelsea - West Ham match," recalls Brian Kelson. "It was the first football match I'd been to on my own, me and three mates. Everybody seemed to have crombies on. The Shed was full of crombies. It kicked off, and it was just electrifying and that exciting, going off everywhere. The West Ham fans had got into The Shed, and then the police came up, and it was fighting with them. I remember sitting down at half time and there were four or five lads in front of us, pulling things out of their crombies, and they all had tools, knives and that. When I left school, I went back down there and it had all changed, but up the back were half a dozen lads in brogues, red tags and tonic jackets, so I got talking to them. I used to go down every week and meet them, and there seemed to be more of us every week."

Hooliganism at football games continued throughout the Seventies, despite better crowd control and the threat of jail sentences which replaced the usual fine or the even more usual kick up the arse by a plod as you were booted out of the ground, free to go on your merry way.

The late Seventies and early Eighties saw it return in a big way however, first with the new breed of skinheads and then with the casuals, many of whom had been skinheads but no longer wanted to be associated with the police's dated idea of what a hooligan was. 1980 doesn't seem that long ago, but most people seem to have forgotten just how violent life was then.

Easter bank holiday weekend that year summed it up. As well as trouble between rival youth cults at seaside resorts around the British Isles, trouble at football games was rife because of the tradition of holding derby games on bank holidays to guarantee big crowds. At White Hart Lane, a Spurs fan threw a petrol bomb at rival Arsenal fans, and in Cardiff more than 50 arrests were made as 300 police officers tried to stop the running battles that followed Cardiff City's 1-0 win over Swansea City.

As far as seaside towns were concerned, Southend drew the short straw. It is a traditional bank holiday haunt for Londoners, and over a thousand skinheads ended up there, looking for rockers and mods to do battle with. To make matters worse, Southend United were at home to Millwall. Brighton and Margate saw skinhead and mod violence and the two towns clocked up over 100 arrests between them. Other towns by the coast from Oban up in Scotland to Weston-Super-Mare on the South West Coast saw varying levels of violence, as did numerous football grounds.

"People say they don't understand why they do all this," says Brian Kelson when talking about football violence. "Well people saying that, and these are top people – politicians, whatever – saying that they can't understand it, well that's just ignorance. If you don't understand something then you're ignorant of it. You're uneducated."

"Violence is part and parcel of being young," argues Paul Jameson. "Whether you're a skinhead, a mod, a raver or whatever, it's part and parcel of being young."

"Violence is part of growing up, it's part of every teenager growing up," agrees Watford Jon. "You can't escape it, it's part of life."

To some extent that's true, but there are a lot of people out there who don't grow up in the urban jungle, who don't go out looking for a fight every Saturday night, who can't understand what the hell is happening when gangs from opposite ends of the country are willing to travel hundreds of miles to fight each other in and around football grounds. To them, the violence is senseless, pointless, mindless.

Sociologists are always looking for ways to explain football hooliganism and other forms of youth violence. Most will conveniently blame social factors like poor housing, unemployment, lack of amenities for the trouble, but they are really missing the point. Violence, whether it's Rambo doing the business with a sub-machine gun on the big screen, or football fans ambushing rival fans at a train station, is all about entertainment. Violence is exciting, dangerous, frightening, exhilarating, hilarious at times – in fact everything good entertainment should be. It's not everybody's idea of a good night out, but neither is the opera, dog racing or bingo. It's horses for courses, and there's no doubting that a lot of young males get a buzz, get an adrenaline rush, get their kicks out of organised violence and the bravado and excitement that accompanies it – even if nothing happens. None of this is meant as an excuse, just some sort of explanation.

And like a drug, it can become addictive. What's more, a crowd seems to take on a life of its own once things start to liven up, and the tendency is to get carried away by it all. As Irvine Welsh puts it in Marabou Stork Nightmares, swallow the fear and feel the buzz.

"The place we used to get the most trouble was at the local team, Wolves," reckons Brian. Wolves, of course, play at Molineaux and, even to this day, Harry J Allstars' reggae classic Liquidator is played before the start of every home game. "I started going there, and it used to be the North Bank, and then the fans stopped going there and went to the South Bank, but the police there were just mad for it. I remember at half-time, below the South Bank where you got your Oxo and crisps and what have you, there always seemed to be trouble. It always seemed to be the police versus whoever was about. I remember standing up the North Bank and the ball went into the crowd and the fans wouldn't give it back. So three or four police came into the crowd and someone shouting something at them. They looked over and grabbed me! They took me up the back, gave me a right good kicking on the floor, nicked my watch and threw me out on the street. At that age, 16-17, I didn't think anything of it – it's just a story to tell your mates."

In 1969, the BBC's Man Alive documentary series made a programme entitled, What's The Truth About Hell's Angels And Skinheads? The first half was devoted to a gang of Angels from Birmingham who came across as a pale imitation of their American forerunners. They were little more than ordinary greasers, looking to shock old grannies with their scruffy appearance and Nazi regalia. No wonder the skinheads hated them. One of the Angels, who called himself Hitler (scary!) boasted that one way to prove yourself as a Hell's Angel was to "beat a skinhead up, that's class. If it were legal, we'd go around hanging skinheads." Our mate Hitler would have had problems hanging out the washing, let alone anything else, the dirty bastard.

The skinheads featured were from London. A few were filmed at Chelsea where 1,000 skins regularly attended home games. Others were from the East End, and they ridiculed the Hell's Angels and talked about fighting the greasers and bashing pakis. Interestingly enough, all said it had nothing to do with the colour of their skin, and all said they had Jamaican friends and mixed with them no problem – in fact, the Jamaicans hated pakis too. The documentary made it quite clear that both cults were expected to be short-lived, little more than current fashions that would last a few years longer at best.

At the time, when they filmed Chelsea skinheads away at Newcastle United, nobody would have thought that over 25 years later, another skinhead documentary would be made, this time with footage of skinheads at a football game, not in Britain, but in Berlin. Surprisingly, despite its size and importance as a city, Berlin does not boast a big name football team. The local derby game between Union Berlin and Berliner FC was played out in front of a crowd of around 5,000 and in a ground that wouldn't have been out of place in the English Third Division. Berliner FC was the team of the old East German secret police, the Stasi, and so their popularity does not extend much beyond their own support. They are still a bigger club than Union Berlin though, and boast a hooligan firm, which includes fascist skinheads, of around 200, compared to Union's mob of around 50, which includes non-political skins.

In so many ways, it was like time-travelling back to the pre-casual days of British terrace aggro. The Union hooligans met at a station a few stops away from the ground to gather their numbers – numbers that didn't quite materialise as had hoped. What's more, police officers were at the station, watching what train they were going to take and generally letting it be known that they had sussed the situation.

Alcohol usually fuels the appetite for aggro (although you might be surprised by the large number of hooligans who don't drink, preferring a clear head should things get lively), but on this day it seemed to have the opposite effect. It looked as if Union would be heavily outnumbered if trouble started and so, after a beer or two, it was decided to go to the game, but only just before kick-off time. Another beer later, the decision was made to go to the game just after it had started so as to avoid the Berliner FC mob before the game. One more beer, and the decision was taken to not go to the game after all, watch it in a pub, and then turn up when nobody was expecting them.

In the end, they made it to the game just after kick-off, and found themselves heavily outnumbered all right – by the police. There must have been as many Old Bill at the game as both hooligan mobs put together, and the police had the distinct advantage of being armed. The chance of aggro after the game was non-existent, not within the immediate vicinity of the ground anyway. For anything serious to have happened, it would have had to be planned to take place well away from the ground itself.

That said, a small group of Berliner FC hooligans did scale the fence and run the full length of the pitch during the second half to confront the Union fans, catching the police totally by surprise. One of the Union skinheads also managed to walk all the way around the ground to pull down a big flag that said SCHEISS UNION ("Union Shit"), and after being grabbed by the police, he managed to talk his way free by saying he was actually French (which he was) and was only looking for his friends!

Those who wonder why people fight at football and then add, "It's only a game" are also totally missing the point. Football just happens to be the perfect arena for violence. The passion is certainly there and the football club acts as a focus for local pride and as a magnet for youths willing to defend its honour. Most importantly though, it offers the opportunity to travel all over the country to fight like-minded mobs and gives you the opportunity to entertain them on your own patch.

Football hooliganism almost exists in a parallel life to the game itself. Violence has home and away and even Cup fixtures – getting a result is all important, losing face means anything from dropping a few points on a good day to being relegated or even put out of business on a bad one. There's even some movement between mobs, a sort of free transfer market.

Banning football wouldn't stop the violence. In fact, banning pubs would do most to empty hospital casualty departments on a Saturday night, but nobody ever suggests that. Too much money involved. In fact, the only reason football hooliganism is seen as a problem is because it takes away from the family game reputation that generates millions for those who live off the backs of the people's game.

If it wasn't for football, the violence would just appear elsewhere. Humans, and particularly males, are aggressive animals, end of story. When Madness played in Edinburgh in 1993, the violence that erupted before they went on stage was the worst seen at a gig for many a year, and illustrated the potential for what would normally be considered football-related violence to transfer itself elsewhere. In fact, thanks to close circuit TV and police tactics, football grounds and other traditional flashpoints like train stations and underground stations are seeing less and less aggro, and it's taking place away from the watchful eye of Big Brother.

Why the trouble started at the Madness gig doesn't really matter, but it offers an insight as to why skinheads and similar gangs are so readily associated with violence. The fact is that the bond within a skinhead gang or a football mob is strong enough to make people want to stand rather than run. And with that comes power. And with power comes the desire to wield it, to prove who is the best.

At the Madness gig, the Capital City Service provided another awesome display of violence that has made Hibs casuals the most feared crew in Scottish football, and one of the most notorious mobs in Britain. The fact that those involved were mainly from their younger ranks made it all the more impressive. Their success depended not so much on numerical superiority – they had maybe 150 boys tops in a crowd of 8,000 – but because they were fighting for something far more important than a spilled beer. Every time the CCS chant went up, they became as one and charged into anyone who wanted to know.

On the receiving end were hooligans from other teams (Airdrie's Section B were well-represented and there were a few boys from Motherwell's Saturday Service involved too), but they were outnumbered by the CCS and severely hampered by ordinary gig goers who kept getting in the way. Then, of course, you had quite a few blokes who just fancied a scrap, didn't have a clue who they were fighting, and ended up lashing out at anyone and everyone, or taking kickings from casuals from different mobs.

Despite the large presence of skinheads at the gig, very few were involved in the trouble and the main reason for that was that most had gone with a few mates and not as crews. The strength and power comes from being together with others you know and trust, and those that joined in the trouble as individuals were either drunk, stupid or aggro junkies.

The gig violence also illustrated the comical and the dark side of violence. Wee Ian, who was one of the Glasgow Spy Kids, was at the bar when the trouble kicked-off, and he managed to weave his way through 200 or so fighting bodies without spilling a drop of the beer he was carrying. People were getting hit over the head with fire extinguishers and scaffolding poles, and he walked the full length of the action without a hair out of place. After the gig though, I heard that a pregnant girl had been kicked to the ground and had lost her baby as a result of the attack. Maybe violence isn't always all it's cracked up to be after all.

Violence has and probably always will be associated with both football and the skinhead cult. And deservedly so too, given the cult's history, but that doesn't mean that all skinheads are violent and it doesn't mean that only skinheads are violent. It also doesn't mean that all violence involving skinheads was started by skinheads either, but still the myth remains that skinheads are trouble no matter what. As the saying goes, when skins do anything good it isn't remembered, but when skins do anything bad, it's never forgotten.

"It's not just skinheads who fight," says Phil, a black skinhead from New York who plays drums for The Templars and virtually every other Oi! band in the Big Apple. "Metalheads fight, hippies fight over pot, everyone fights. It's just skinheads are always tagged."

We live in a violent society and violence makes the news. For skinheads it's almost the only time they make the news and so the media picture is of a cult constantly involved in violence. In reality, it's only a small part of what the cult has to offer, and you can be a skinhead for years and never raise a hand in anger.

"I wouldn't say it was a particularly violent cult," reckons Jacquel, "but people have portrayed it that way, yes. The male going to football, having a fight kind of thing. But for me, violence isn't a part of it."

"The look's an extreme look", says Big Iain. "With boots and a shaved head, it's hard to look nice and quiet. You look nasty whether you are or not. It's a predominantly violent-looking cult. The media seem intent on making skinheads the number one violent cult, and even now when skinheads are few and far between, they still portray the nasty villains as skinheads."

The media, of course, has played its part in attracting people to the skinhead cult who see it as an outlet for the violence that they have within them.

"Violence is part of life, not just the cult," points out Gail, the Coventry FC skingirl in exile in County Durham. "There's always going to be morons no matter what you're involved in and so some skinheads are going to be violent, but it's not part of the criteria for being a skinhead."

Skinhead's reputation for aggro is part of the attraction of the cult for a lot of youngsters. When you are a kid of 12 or 13, and people are getting out of your way just because you have a shaved head and a pair of boots on, it makes you feel good. You've also got a lot to live up to, especially when you're with mates, and so skinheads tend not to back away from trouble as often as they probably should do. It's all about face and not losing it. And while the look certainly discourages some people from crossing you, it also seems to attract some real nutters who want to have a go to prove how hard they are.

"One time, I went to jail and it was all over the news – three Nazi skins arrested and guns found and all that," says Chris of his days with the United White Skins in Maryland. "I got beat by the whole unit. I had stitches all over my face, and it was like they obviously wanted me to be attacked. Like they put me in a unit with 15 blacks and left my cell door unlocked."

Skinheads tend to have the advantage of numbers because of the gang mentality that is part and parcel of the cult. Skinheads in general have an incredible belief in loyalty to their friends, and when a fight breaks out the chances are your mates will be straight in there with you.

"There was 25 or 30 of us, and we'd been together for about ten years, and over those ten years, you become so close that you really are your own little army," says Symond of his days as a Wycombe skin. "We knew that when violent situations did arise, you would be together. There'd be at least five or six of you that would fight to the death, and I know that sounds really extreme but because you were hated so much by everybody – by your parents, your school teachers, by the police, by everybody – it drew you so close together that you became as one."

"If I have a problem with you, I will deal with it in a way I feel necessary," says another Chris, this time a skinhead of Filipino decent from New York. "If I don't like you and you say something that offends me, I'll kick your head in. What skinheads have is unified power. If I knew a person, just one person, and that person got hit, all the skinheads would have to fight it out for him."

Asian Chris appeared in the World Of Skinhead documentary, and one of the clips showed him squaring up to a bloke with a big mouth and then walking away. The clip was intended to illustrate the point that sometimes it takes a bigger man to walk away from trouble than it does to stand and fight, but the way it was cut together in the programme made it look like he talked a good fight, and then didn't back it up with action.

What actually happened though was that we had been filming an interview when the bloke had walked past on his way home from the pub, and he started shouting abuse. Chris was willing to go ahead with him, but it was me that walked over and said forget it, let's just get on with the filming. Chris walked away and the other bloke didn't complain – until we had walked fifty yards and then he started shouting again about going home to get his gun to shoot us (we later heard he actually did come back half an hour later with a gun, but we'd luckily finished and gone home by then!).

If the fight had gone ahead, the mouth would have taken a kicking if for no other reason than he was on his own and Chris wasn't. To me, we had travelled thousands of miles to make a documentary, not to start fights in the street. If anyone lost face that night, it was me – but since I don't have to live in New York, I couldn't have cared less.

The following night, we were at a ska gig, having a good time, when a couple of drunken arseholes started to pick on a bloke who was with us, and who wasn't a skinhead or a fighter either. After seeing what was happening, I just tapped Asian Chris on the shoulder without even looking at him, and stepped in to help out the bloke being bullied. I'd only met Asian Chris a few times, but such is the bond between skinheads that I instinctively knew he would turn around, see what was happening and back me up. In the event, Asian Chris came steaming past me and ended up wading in first. Only a few punches were thrown before the morons backed away. Nobody got badly hurt because they didn't want to mess with skinheads, knowing that there were another 20 or so inside the gig and around 40 outside. That's what Chris means by unified power. And Chris was straight in there when it mattered without giving it a second thought.

It's dangerous to romanticise about violence. No matter how necessary, the end result is somebody gets hurt and the risk is that somebody is you. And the higher the stakes, the higher the risks. Every year, a handful of skinheads die in street fights that more often than not involve rival skinhead gangs.

"There are instances where you have to defend yourself and stick up for your mates," says Chicago skinhead Perry, "and sometimes you have to do what you have to do, but I think, generally, the movement would be a whole lot better off if people thought more with their brains and less with their boots."

No One Likes Us

At the start of December 1991, 200 skinheads marched through the streets of Lübeck in Germany. The March Of The Skinheads was organised by the Lübeck Bootboys and Bootgirls to protest against the fact that the media was constantly blaming skinheads for the rise in neo-Nazi activity which sharply increased following the reunification of Germany in October, 1990. SKINHEADS – BUT NOT RACISTS was the message on the huge banner that was carried at the front of the demonstration.

It was an important day for the skinhead cult in Germany, even if it was to be totally swallowed up and lost in the events that preceded the march and those that followed. The world's spotlight turned on Germany in horror as pictures of gangs of neo-Nazis attacking hostels for refugees, often cheered on by older people, filled TV screens around the globe.

In November 1992, a grandmother and two young girls were killed in a firebomb attack in Moelln, near Hamburg. Television news reports carried pictures of frightened and defenceless immigrants being besieged by what commentators regularly referred to as "skinheads" – even though the pictures on the screen told a different story. Some of the youths involved in the attacks were indeed skinheads, but the majority had longer hair and weren't dressed in anything remotely close to skinhead fashion.

Again, the focus was on the minority skinhead element which formed a small, vocal, and easily identifiable part of a much larger movement. Again the implication was that all skinheads in Germany were Nazis.

In May 1993, five more Turks – two women and three children – were burned alive in another hideous firebombing, this time in Solingen. Four skinheads were responsible, bringing further shame to the cult. There can be no justification for murdering women and children while they sleep in their beds at night. The people responsible for such attacks, skinheads or otherwise, are the scum of the Earth and a great advertisement for the return of capital punishment.

 For skinheads in Germany, and particularly those with no racist affiliations, things could hardly have been worse. The majority of people had only really heard of skinheads in connection with the increase in racist violence, and in the eyes of both the media and the general public, every skinhead was a potential firebomber, a potential murderer.

Perhaps, you have to walk down the street – the morning after a bout of media hysteria about skinheads – with a cropped head and boots, to fully appreciate how much hatred can be directed at you for belonging to a youth cult. The vast majority of skinheads, irrespective of where they stand politically, were angry and ashamed that the greatest of all youth cults could be associated with anything so horrific, both by those skinheads involved and by sections of the media who had once again used the skinhead folk devil to spice up news reports.

Following the attacks, a number of skinheads who had supported the racist cause beforehand would have nothing more to do with it. A German skinhead band who had been associated with the right-wing also threw in the towel after releasing a single expressing their own disgust at what had happened. Ingo Hasselbach, one of Berlin's leading Nazi skinheads who featured widely in world press reports on the rise of neo-Nazism in Germany, was perhaps the most prominent figure to leave the movement following the deaths. He has since written the book, Führer-Ex - Memoirs Of A Former Neo-Nazi (Chatto & Windus), and now speaks out against the extreme right in Germany.

Führer-Ex is a good book in many ways. It perfectly illustrates the alternative world that extremists of every persuasion create for themselves, a world virtually detached from mainstream society where your beliefs are reinforced by those around you, and the siege mentally such detachment creates. It also shows the attractions and fascinations in what becomes, literally, a way of life.

Hasselbach's involvement with the skinhead cult can be traced back to him growing up in the totalitarian East Germany. To speak out against the Communist regime earned you a prison sentence, and few forms of protest existed to young people beyond being a hippy, a punk or a skinhead. At the time, those that the state media called "neo-Nazis" were really just people who totally resented living under such an oppressive regime, and that was especially true of the skinheads.

For those living in the West, it is hard to imagine what life is like under communist rule, but the fact that as a skinhead you would be jailed for simply chanting "Oi! Oi! Oi!" in a public place gives some idea of how restrictive life could be. One skinhead got two and a half years for just that offence.

Given the way the media has focused so heavily on the skinhead involvement in the rise of neo-Nazism in Germany, you would expect Ex-Führer to be full of references to the cult. It isn't. Indeed, despite shaving his own head and wearing army boots, Hasselbach himself shows no real interest in the cult. In one of the few references he makes to skinheads, he dismisses them in a sentence as "the idiots who cleared the streets for us and intimidated our enemies".

It's also clear that the majority of neo-Nazis weren't skinheads anyway, and more than once they had to rely on football hooligans for extra muscle – casuals who were attracted more by the violence and the potential for looting than they ever were by the politics.

Not only then did the media distort the coverage of events in Germany in the early 1990s, but Hasselbach also states that the media attention increased his National Alternative party's bank account five-fold – as money from new members and the press came pouring in. The media paid for interviews and photo opportunities – Hitler salutes cost extra – and the extensive coverage given to groups like the National Alternative served as the most effective recruitment tool the extreme right had at its disposal.

On Thursday, 16th of January, 1996, ten people were killed when fire swept through a hostel housing foreigners in the German port city of Lübeck. Arson was thought to have been the cause and three youths from the area were arrested in connection with the fire. This horrific tragedy again made the headlines around the world, and here in Britain it was reported that the three youths were "connected to the local skinhead scene" – all the proof that was needed to pass a guilty verdict in a lot of people's minds.

Anti-fascist demonstrations were held in Lübeck and Hamburg, and once again skinheads were Germany's public enemy number one. Just days later, there was an important breakthrough in the case – only, chances are, you missed it because it wasn't front page news anymore. The three youths had been released without being charged. They had nothing to do with the fire. A Lebanese refugee who lived with his family in the hostel was charged with arson.

If he deliberately started the fire, rotting in hell would be too good for him. But there'll be no more demonstrations. Ten dead in a fire, but unless there are political points to be scored, very few people seem to care.

There's no getting away from the fact that some of those involved in the increase in racially-motivated crimes in Germany were and are skinheads. Among them, you'll have committed skinheads, kids who don't have a clue what skinhead is all about, and people who are right-wing, want people to know they are right-wing and so adopt the look of the stereotypical racist. Add them together and you still don't get the majority of those involved. And just because some of those involved in the arson attacks happened to be skinheads, that doesn't mean that all German skinheads want to see the establishment of a Fourth Reich. Not by a long chalk. And even those skinheads who do want to see a Germany free of Turks and other immigrants don't necessarily agree with firebombing.

It is possible to hold racist views without supporting racial violence. The media though, in its quest for thirty second sound bites, nearly always portrays it as if it is only skinheads that are responsible for the attacks, and that all skinheads are therefore guilty by association. They may not always intend that to be the case, but that's how it comes over.

"I know how the media portrays skinheads and I don't like it," said reggae star, Judge Dread, at the time of the hostel attacks. "I work a lot in Germany and I work mainly for the skinheads out there. Just because skinheads wear boots and braces doesn't mean they are bad. Al Capone wore a suit and tie, the Mafia wear suits and ties, so you can't judge people by their dress, but they always assume that skinheads are bad. The nasty, snarling skinhead. I go to Germany and I talk to the skinheads there and they're into the music and they're not racial – how can they be racial when they're into black music? You hear all these stories about skinheads doing this and skinhead violence, and I think, hold on a minute, this doesn't happen where I work. All the skinheads that I've met have been non-violent and non-racist, and they make a point of letting it be known that they are. They run rallies and all sorts of things there, and they even give money to charity."

The first skinheads in Germany were British soldiers who took the style over during the days of Sham and 2 Tone. Skinheads have always been well-represented in the armed forces and it's only natural that they take their music, civvie street clothes, and such like with them on their travels.

To begin with, German skinheads only appeared in towns and cities that had a British army base, but by the early Eighties, the cult had spread to towns with no British influences. Again, at the start the cult was very British in character – right down to German skins wearing Union Jacks and West Ham football tops – but as time went on, the German skinheads found their own identity.

"The skinhead way of life came to Germany as an already distorted kind of movement because the National Front had already had some impact on the movement in England," says Emma Steel. "So when it came to Germany, it was distorted, and there were a lot of people thinking, 'I'm right-wing so I have to dress up like a skinhead'."

Most countries on mainland Europe seem to be more politicised than the British Isles. People tend to be more politically active and motivated in countries like Germany, Spain, and Italy than they ever are here, and this is reflected in youth culture too.

In the early Eighties, the German punk scene became closely associated with the country's squatter movement and other left-wing causes, and so those punks who wanted to distance themselves from the left-wing turned to the skinhead cult. Within a few years, it was generally true that punks were left-wing in Germany and skinheads were right-wing, and this was true for both West Germany and East Germany. When Peter & The Test Tube Babies played there around this time, they were confronted by 800 sieg heiling skinheads.

There were exceptions though and a number of German skinheads had no interest in right-wing politics, preferring to support the left-wing or take no interest in politics whatsoever. When Skinheads Against Racial Prejudice was imported to Europe from the States by The Oppressed's Roddy Moreno in the late Eighties, its message found fertile ground in Germany, and SHARP quickly established a sizeable presence among German skinheads. By the late Eighties, it had been firmly established that not all skinheads were racist, and that you could become a skinhead without having to subscribe to anything remotely resembling national socialism.

Further boost to the ranks of the non-racist skinheads came from a rapidly growing ska scene, based on the early success of bands like Skaos, The Braces, The Busters, and Blechreiz. If you were a skinhead who enjoyed listening to what was black music, it made little sense to also support the extreme right, and a number of ska bands took it upon themselves to openly oppose racism and encouraged their followers to do likewise.

In 1989, Pork Pie Records was launched by a Berlin skin called Matzge to act as a home for the burgeoning ska scene that, to this day, attracts hundreds of skinheads every year to major ska festivals held in towns like Potsdam and Aachen. In fact, together with the USA, Germany is a true focus for the underground ska scene as it is today, and regularly plays host to full tours by bands like Bad Manners and The Selecter, as well as home grown talent too. What's more, it is one of the few countries where old ska and reggae stars get to perform on a regular basis in front of large appreciative audiences – audiences full of skinheads.

The media makes great play out of the fact that hundreds of skins turn out to see neo-Nazi bands perform, but rarely mention the fact that similar numbers of skins can be found at ska gigs.

"Their love of the early music amazes me," says Judge Dread. "Last year at Potsdam, I was on stage at the same time as Derrick Morgan, Laurel Aitken, Justin Hinds, and Rico. That probably wouldn't happen here."

The creation of a united Germany, and the upsurge in nationalist sentiment that accompanied it, did much to swell the ranks of the extreme right, especially when promises of a better life failed to materialise in the East, and the West was left to pick up the massive cost of unification. This, in turn, led to an increase in political extremism and racism, with immigrants being blamed for the country's economic problems.

Up until then, SHARP had managed to achieve some positive media coverage for the skinhead cult, but you can only do so much to shift public opinion. It soon became impossible to combat the images of burning hostels, and so SHARP became more or less ineffective. A recent opinion poll said that just 2% of the German population would want to share Christmas with a skinhead, such is the cult's current standing in the public's eyes.

Even so, the skinhead cult remains strong in Germany as a whole. People come and go, but there are certainly no signs of the cult's strength of numbers diminishing. Even so, it is far from united. It's ridiculous to have to continually define skinheads in political terms, but for the sake of outsiders reading this, German skinheads today represent all points on the political spectrum, and it is these political differences that leave the cult divided. That said, it is incredible enough that the cult has survived recent events without expecting it to have done so in one piece.

"Hard times need hard guys," Uli of the Berlin-based Skin Up fanzine says as way of an explanation for the cult's continued existence. "The economic situation is getting worse and if there's no chance of getting a job, it's a lot easier to take on a hard lifestyle."

Berlin is as good a place as any to offer a snapshot of the German skinhead scene. It was – until recently – divided, with West Berlin and East Berlin not so much being a tale of two cities, but a tale of two worlds. West Berlin was an island of Western democracy in a sea of communism and was a vibrant, exciting, potentially dangerous place to be during the Cold War. Naturally, that feeling of living on the edge has faded since the Berlin Wall came down, but in many ways the city remains divided.

Those in former West Berlin have a tendency to still see East Berlin as backward, while East Berliners see their western counterparts as arrogant. For generations, they led such different lives that it will be a good few years before the city is fully integrated again.

There are around 800 skinheads in the city, and they are fairly evenly divided between the east and the west. Although things are slowly changing, the chances are that those living in former West Berlin have little regular contact with those in former East Berlin, except at gigs and similar events. The physical barriers are gone, but the mental ones remain firmly in position.

The Berlin skinhead scene is also divided along political lines. There are large numbers of both Hammerskins and Blut Und Ehre Skins in the city, although they tend to be concentrated in the south and south west. Together, they represent the neo-Nazi and racist elements and share little in common with other skinheads in the city beyond the name. There are also still a large number of SHARP skins in the city, mainly in the West, although their numbers have fallen for the same reason SHARP has declined in other areas – its ineffectiveness, left-wing infiltration, and the fact that skinheads themselves know the score and have no desire to pander to the wishes of outsiders. There are also a small number of redskins and anarchist skins, but both are a very small minority. The remaining skinheads are non-political, those who choose to put their love of the skinhead way of life above all politics.

The largest gang of non-political skins in the city are the Prenzlauerberg Oi! Skins who come mainly from the Prenzlauerberg district of what was East Berlin. The Prenzlauerberg Oi! Skins number around 50 or 60 and came together in 1994 from the remnants of a number of other gangs. Before e fall of the Wall, most skinheads in East Germany were right-wing as a direct result of living under communist regime, but not many had much idea of what the skinhead cult was really about. It was ifficult to get authentic skinhead clothing too so they had to make do with what they could find.

he united Germany did see an upsurge in support for the extreme right-wing, but at the same time, large numbers of former East German skins either offered their support to SHARP or saw that politics played no part in the cult and adopted a non-political stance. In a society where skinheads are either left-wing or right-wing or not entitled to an opinion, it leaves the likes of the Prenzlauerberg Oi! Skins to more or less stand alone.

"We get attacked by both sides, by SHARP and right-wing skins too, so we really stand on our own," explains Jenny, a skingirl from the gang.

While the extreme right skinheads have their own music scene, SHARP skins and non-political skinheads tend to share a love for ska, reggae, Oi! and the like, and so tend to mix together. In effect, this creates the two skinhead factions that are repeated throughout the world. On one hand, you have the racist, nationalist, and Nazi skinheads who gravitate towards the white power scene; and, on the other hand, you have the non-political, SHARP, and left-wing skinheads who have broadly similar musical tastes as mentioned earlier and who tend to be either non-racist or anti-racist.

Of course, you can hold virtually any political stance or have no political stance and still see racism as wrong.

"Most of the non-racist skins are not at all political, and that's an important point because when you tell people that there are anti-racist skinheads, they immediately think they are left-wing which is complete nonsense," says Emma Steel.

There is a slight overlap between the two big factions, but that is becoming smaller as the issue of racism has polarised the cult's two wings. In the mid-Eighties, it wasn't too unusual for a skinhead to go to a Skrewdriver concert one week and a ska gig the following week. It wasn't a regular occurrence, but it did happen more then than it does now.

"Everyone has their own political opinions within the Prenzlauerberg Oi! Skins," explains Alex, who is Jenny's older brother, "but it's down to private individuals, just as it should be."

Of course, there are those on the right-wing who assume that because the Prenzlauerberg crew does not support them, the term non-political really means left-wing. And there will be those on the left-wing who continually accuse non-political skins of being fascist appeasers or closet right-wing skinheads. It's always difficult for the politically motivated to believe that you might genuinely believe that politics has nothing to do with being a skinhead and so are not interested in playing their petty games. That's as true in Berlin as it is anywhere else in the world.

"By calling myself non-racist, not only am I against the Nazis and the Klan and shit like that," says Pete from New York, "I'm also against shit like the Nation Of Islam and that Malcolm X bullshit. It's the same thing, it's just a different colour. Minority racism, blacks hate the whites, blacks hate the Jews, Jews hate the blacks, whatever – it's the same thing. It's all bullshit, white supremacy or black supremacy."

The Prenzlauerberg crew are regularly accused of being Nazis, firstly because they are skinheads, secondly because they are from East Berlin, and thirdly because they don't support SHARP. They are proud of their country too and cannot understand why so many people confuse their patriotism with Nazism, but their pride in themselves and their country does not extend to prejudice. Within the gang, there are skinheads who originally come from France, Bulgaria, Hungary, and Mongolia, and all are accepted without question.

Alex and Jenny themselves are Jews, something that isn't a problem as far as being a skinhead goes, but does cause trouble at home.

"Our parents don't like us being skinheads very much because our religion is Jewish and they think the two don't fit together. They tolerate it, but seeing us walking around in boots makes them wonder what others will think of us because of the way the media portrays skinheads as evil, the lowest of the low."

"The media frees people from their own racism," argues Alex, "because they can look at us and say 'You're the racists.'"

Some people might be surprised that Alex and Jenny don't support SHARP, but they prefer to side with the non-political cause. Being anti-racist is a moral issue for them, and they have no need to prove it by the wearing of a badge.

"The basic idea of SHARP is right and we agree with that," says Alex of the Prenzlauerberg Oi! Skins in general, "but we just don't see why we should enter this movement because we just can't get along with some of the leading SHARP skins in West Berlin personally. SHARP has also been used and drawn too much towards the left-wing."

Most SHARP skins will point out that SHARP's only stance is on racism, and any skinheads who oppose racism are welcome to wear the SHARP colours, irrespective of other political beliefs. That's the theory, but in practice, the left-wing has attempted to use SHARP as its own political foot soldiers with varying degrees of success.

Even so, in Berlin, those in the anarchist movement and on the extreme left still seem all too willing to believe that anything associated with the skinhead cult must be Nazi by definition. And that included French ska band, Skarface, who toured Germany, but were told their last gig in Berlin was cancelled because the band were suspected of being right-wing sympathisers.

They could have gone home, but instead travelled to Berlin to confront their accusers and to ask for the gig to go ahead. After explaining the reality of a band whose motto is "100% ska, 200% fun", Skarface were told to return to the venue in an hour's time for a final decision. When they came back, they were attacked with baseball bats and metal bars, and several of the band members needed hospital treatment. To their credit, it was the SHARP skins who were outraged by the events that had taken place, and publicised the facts in the pages of Skin Up in the hope that other bands would boycott the promoters and venue.

West Berlin holds few attractions for the Prenzlauerberg Oi! Skins, but they travel there en masse for gigs. Cock Sparrer's visit to Berlin in March 1995 attracted skinheads from all over the city, despite the fact that the gig was held in an area with a high Turkish population. The reality was that there was no trouble between local youths and the skinheads attending the gig, but the perceived threat of trouble is just as important as the reality of a situation, and some skins preferred to wait until Sparrer returned to play what was considered a safer part of town rather than venture into a Turkish part of the city. It may seem paranoid, but thanks to media hysteria and left-wing agitation, gigs in certain parts of the city have the potential of becoming Germany's Southall.

Of course, local Turkish gangs aren't interested in what music Sparrer or any other band plays. They just see hundreds of skinheads coming to their part of town and, like most other people, they believe what the media tells them about skinheads.

In fact, a classic case of media hysteria involved a Turkish journalist and the Berlin SHARP skins. The journalist stayed with one of the skinheads while he spent time talking to the SHARP crew and following them around the city. The very fact that a Turkish journalist was welcomed into the home of a skinhead, together with the blatant anti-racist stance of the skinheads he met, should have resulted in some positive coverage for those involved, but incredibly that was not the case. The journalist sold his story to a Turkish magazine, claiming he had gone undercover with Nazi skinheads, and he simply invented fairy tale comments to go along with the article that had swastikas on every page for added effect. It's little wonder that there is trouble in Germany between skinheads and Turkish street gangs, and it's equally no surprise that skinheads trust journalists as far as they can kick them.

"The media have their own prejudices and most of them don't really want to know about the skinhead movement," says Emma Steel who was involved in the above incident. "They just want their prejudices to come true. And if you give interviews and they are not coming true, they will find a way to put it into a context to make people believe that all skinheads really are Nazis."

One of the Prenzlauerberg Oi! Skins summed up perfectly the German media's use of scapegoats when he said, "For AIDS, they blame gay people. For unemployment, it's the foreigners. And for racism, it's us."

The Cock Sparrer gig was a shining example of why being a skinhead is worth all the grief you get. No other band can knock out three minute street classics that perfectly capture the reality of life on such a consistent basis. Songs like Argy Bargy, The Sun Says, Because You're Young, Chip On Your Shoulder, Get A Rope, Bird Trouble, Where Are They Now, Sunday Stripper, Take 'Em All, Riot Squad, Watch Your Back, and perhaps a dozen more are street anthems without match. It's criminal that Cock Sparrer isn't topping the charts every other month, but such is the stitched up world we live in.

When Sparrer launch into England Belongs To Me, four or five hundred German skinheads join in with the chorus. A number of German skins still wear Union Jack patches, either to show their allegiance to British street music or to show respect for the birthplace of their youth cult. Let's see the sociologists explain that one away with their oh-so-clever theories. Not only do you have British Nazi skinheads who worship Adolf Hitler, but you have German skinheads with no interest in Nazism who proudly wear the Union Jack on their jackets.

Sparrer's Riot Squad could have been dedicated to the reception party that was waiting for the skinheads as the gig came to an end. Across the street from the venue, a long row of police vans was waiting, its occupants decked out in full riot gear. The German skinheads call the police "the green shadow" because they constantly monitor skinhead activity, although, like most outsiders, they don't differentiate between the different breeds of skinhead. Berlin also suffers from the fact that jobs had to be found for former border guards, the secret police, and other potential misfits, and so the city boasts a large police force with time on its hands.

As the skinheads poured out onto the street, their only interest was in finding a bus home. The police though were obviously anticipating trouble, and when it wasn't forthcoming they were quite happy to try and provoke it.

Around ten skinheads and skingirls from the Prenzlauerberg mob were standing on a street corner, waiting for the traffic lights to change so that they could cross the road and find their transport home. As they stood there, minding their own business, a police van drove past, slowed down, and sprayed the skinheads with CS gas. A skingirl and her skinhead boyfriend caught the full force of it, leaving both in temporary agony as their eyes burned with the pain. The police van then turned around and parked on the opposite side of the street, waiting for a reaction. On this occasion, the skinheads didn't rise to it, and the presence of a TV camera – which unintentionally captured the event on film – no doubt discouraged the police from raising the stakes further.

On another night though, you would have had a riot on your hands and you don't need two guesses to know who would have been blamed in the newspapers the next day. ACAB.

Being a skinhead in Germany is a far from easy path to walk, irrespective of your political views, but it remains a country that boasts arguably the largest skinhead scene of today. A large part of its survival against all odds is the virtual self-sufficiency of the scene – tours, gigs, record labels, even clothing suppliers are generally run and organised by skinheads, ex-skinheads, band members or other people with a genuine feel and love for what they are doing. That German knack for organisation is certainly paying dividends here anyway.

For a number of years now, Germany has also been home to a large selection of quality skinhead fanzines so there is little need to rely on the mainstream media for help.

"The normal media doesn't even give normal youths what they need," argues Uli. "There are a lot of publications for young people, but most of them are bullshit. And this is especially true for skinheads because you'll never read about bands we like and what's important to us, so we have to do it on our own."

Outsiders understandably see skinhead as a fashion. For some, that's no doubt the case, but few people appreciate the depth of feeling skinheads have for their cult. To many, it comes close to being a religion and adversity just makes those beliefs all the more stronger. Nowhere is that truer than in Germany. They may not be able to trace their roots back to the late Sixties like British skins can, but they are fighting tooth and nail for the pride and dignity that has always been part of the skinhead cult. As Alex says, "Skinhead is about being very low on the ladder of society, but still making something of your life."

Us And Them

"Skinhead's a way of life, a culture I live by," says Pan from Portland, but it could be any one of thousands of skinheads talking. "It's about having pride in the way I look, it's about working for my living, earning everything I get. It's about the second family I have with my mates on the street, about being true to the values that I learned, the honour code that I learned. It's about all that coming together, and it's the truest culture because you're talking about the real people, the working people, the poor people."

Skinheads are without a doubt a breed apart. Fashion victims come and go in any youth cult, but it takes a certain kind of person to hang on in there through thick and thin. To outsiders, we represent the scum of the Earth, but we know better. We know that we are the part of the greatest youth cult of all time, and nobody can ever take that away from us. It really is us against the world, and, as we know all too well, the world doesn't stand a chance.

There's a skinhead in New York called Donny The Punk. A lot of people on the New York scene will know him as he's often at gigs with notebook in hand, jotting down details for an article that will appear in one fanzine or another. Donny wrote a couple of articles for Skinhead Times and generally kept us up to date with happenings in the Big Apple. He also is running a campaign to get a punk elected president of the United States for some madcap reason or another, but that probably sums up Donny's total commitment to the street music scene.

Beyond that, I don't know a great deal about him except that yesterday I saw him on a CBS Sixty Minutes documentary doing the bravest thing I've ever seen a skinhead do.

Because as well as working hard to promote street and skinhead culture, Donny also runs a small organisation from his New York flat called Stop Prisoner Rape. It offers counselling to victims of prison rape and seeks to educate the public about what is happening to inmates on a daily basis behind prison bars.

They say if you can't do the time, don't do the crime, but life's not always as simple as that. And for one reason or another, a number of skinheads find themselves sewing mail bags in exchange for food and a bed in prisons the world over.

Losing your liberty is bad enough, but other fears play on a man's mind about being sent down. One of the biggest and, ironically, least talked about is the fear of being raped. Just the thought of it conjures up so much shame and disgust, and being the victim of male rape can break the strongest of men.

Inside prisons, male rape rarely has anything to do with homosexuality. It's about power, and the ability to render victims totally powerless. Thanks to the code of silence that exists among prisoners, the fear of reprisals, the devastating shame of being a victim, and the knowledge that the authorities are unlikely to do anything about it anyway, most prison rapes go unreported. Estimates vary, but anything from less than 1% to 12% of the male prison population is raped at one time or another.

Donny was sent to prison after being arrested for trespassing at a demonstration at the White House. On his first night there, he was attacked by five men in his cell who first beat him up and then took it in turn to rape him. He was then dragged from cell to cell where he was repeatedly raped by a further 40 or so inmates. Most people won't even want to begin to imagine the hell he must have gone through during the attack that lasted three hours. Words can't even begin to describe the horrors he must have experienced.

It takes a courageous man to go through something like that and come out the other side with his self-respect. It takes an even braver man to go on TV and tell millions of people exactly what happened to you in the hope that by doing so, you can help other victims of prison rape. The sort of bravery that wins medals on battlefields. The sort of bottle that skinheads throughout the world respect as being part of the very fabric that runs through the skinhead cult in its purest form.

At the time of writing, there are skinheads in Bosnia, Afghanistan and other troubled areas of the world, risking their lives in the armed forces of one country or another to protect the lives of others. There are many other examples of skinheads who are doing brave things, good things, positive things. When you think of them, and skinheads like Donny, the scum of the Earth tag seems a little out of place to say the least. The skinhead cult isn't without its faults, but neither is it the monster so often portrayed by the media and our other enemies.

The reality of the skinhead nation today is that it is a deeply-divided family. The split between skinheads who see themselves as being part of the white power scene and what is basically the rest of the cult is becoming so wide that the chasm is almost unbridgeable.

Personally, I don't judge people on the colour of their skin or their political beliefs and believe that everyone who shaves their head in the name of skinhead has a stake in the skinhead nation. That's not how I'd like it to be in a perfect world, but such is the reality of the situation today.

I've also little doubt that if the gap continues to widen, then the skinhead cult will completely split in two. The only alternative is to accept that every skinhead is entitled to his or her own beliefs as long as they don't ram them down the throats of others, and that outsiders who seek to manipulate skinheads – be they politicians, journalists or whoever – are no longer welcome in our midst.

As things stand, my money's on a divided nation, but only the skinheads of today and tomorrow can decide the cult's ultimate fate. The power really is yours.

For over 30 years now, the skinhead cult has spread throughout the back streets of towns and cities throughout the world. We are the proudest of all youth cults, the finest of all youth cults, the ultimate in youth cults. No amount of media bullshit can ever take that away from us. It's up to the skinheads of today to ensure that the cult lives on by standing proud and by defending the traditions of the skinhead faith. It's important we do it for ourselves, not for outsiders, not for the media, not for politicians. They come and go, but the strong and the true survive.

An Alabama preacher called Martin Luther King once said that he hoped the day would come when his people would be judged by the content of their character, not by the colour of their skin. I too have a small dream. That the people of the skinhead nation will be judged by the content of their character, and not by appearance alone. And that once again, the skinhead nation will stand united, never to be defeated.

Donny The Punk died a few months after the book Skinhead Nation appeared. May he rest in peace.

Printed in Great Britain
by Amazon

44065797R00059